MW01288817

Perfected with Love

A powerful and inspiring true story

Walt Heyer

Dedication

This story was written across decades and through the hearts, hands and prayers of many wonderful people, including, but not limited to the following: Reverend Robert Kraning, former Director of Forest Home Christian Conference Center; the late Dr. Dennis Guernsey, Ph.D., professor and staff psychologist at Fuller Seminary, Pasadena, California; Dr. Roy Thompson and wife Bonita; Jeff Farrar, pastor of Central Peninsula Church; Ed Woodhall, an elder in a large church and his wife Kathy. All of them were moved by the Lord to form the foundation of love that set in motion this great story.

My thanks to Pastor Rick Bailard, Pastor Bob Thune and elder board chairman Don Bennett of Southwest Community Church for the privilege of serving on staff with such an amazing group of dedicated servants such as Catherine Martin, who graciously prepared the forward for this book.

Love and thanks to my wife, Kaycee, and her skill and ability to take my rough drafts to a well-polished finished story.

Love and thanks to my children and all the others who played a part, a big "Thank you."

"Let me give you a new command:
Love one another. In the same way I
loved you, you love one another. This
is how everyone will recognize that
you are my disciples—when they see
the love you have for each other."
John 13:34

Foreword

M any years ago I heard someone say, "If you are looking
for the perfect church, and you think you have found
it; don't join it; you'll ruin it." Most churches are filled with
scraggly, sometimes strange, and often very funny people in
desperate need of mercy, grace, and love.

In *Perfected with Love*, Walt Heyer shows through this
wonderful story, what happens when one person in one
church steps out of the crowd and chooses to love another
into the arms of Jesus and the kingdom of God. We in the
church need to understand and apply this powerful story and
what it teaches about the radical nature of love in action.
Oh, the difference God's unconditional love will make in
the church. His love is the most powerful force in the world.
God's love finds you, saves you, holds you, and keeps you.
And when God's love is expressed through one life to another,
just watch what God does. He makes the impossible possible
and transforms a fledgling life into a beautiful sculpture of
grace and glory.

I have had the privilege to serve with Walt Heyer on
the staff at our church and marvel at how God works in and
through him to touch other lives. He is truly a trophy of God's
grace. Because Walt has experienced the love and grace of
God, he can easily give it away to another. Joseph R. Cooke
writes in his book, *Celebration of Grace*, "Grace is what

love is and does when it meets the sinful and undeserving. It's what enables us to see beyond one another's faults so that we can love one another without reference to whether that love has been earned or deserved. It's what God does when He reaches out in love for us—sinful as we are—and welcomes us into a relationship with Himself."

I encourage you to read *Perfected with Love* and find out how you can make a difference in someone's life in your neighborhood, your church, and perhaps in the world through the application of God's unconditional love.

Catherine Martin
Prolific author, public speaker and founder
of Quiet Time Ministries
April, 2009

Introduction

E very once in a while a story stands out that you just
want to be shared with others. *Perfected with Love* is
just such a story.

The title, *Perfected with Love,* is intended to capture your
imagination. As you will discover, love and its significance
will unfold in every chapter of the story as the Lord unveils
His perfected masterpiece. From start to finish, God's love
is woven into the fabric of this story—special families who
open their homes, churches who open their doors, and so
many individuals who, by their love for Jesus Christ, live out
the truth found in Scripture.

Ephesians 4:2 says "Be completely humble and gentle; be
patient, bearing with one another in love." First Corinthians
13:13 says of faith, hope and love: "The greatest of these is
love."

You will experience a wide range of emotions throughout
the story—excitement, amazement and even tears—as you
discover just how powerful and wonderful the love of Jesus
Christ is. Now get comfortable and come along with me
as we journey along through this amazing story. You will
experience, as I did, God's amazing love for people we often
think of as "scary" and unredeemable.

Chapter 1

The Journey Starts

Her name was Laura, a single woman in her early forties, about to meet Dr. Dennis Guernsey in his office at Fuller Seminary in Pasadena, California. The date—late 1984. Laura walked into the counseling office and gently placed her curvaceous figure on the leather couch across from Dr. Guernsey. Laura loved wearing red sweaters and red lipstick because the bright red color made her blond hair stand out all the more. The warm Southern California day was shining through the window. The bright sunlight lit up the office and the highlights in Laura's hair. It was a beautiful day and she was looking good.

Dennis leaned forward to shake her hand and said, "Hi Laura. Thanks for making the long drive from Ontario."

She nervously smoothed her skirt and replied, "Dennis, this is an important time for me. I came because I want your help in finding a church. I truly feel the need for the comfort of a church family to call home."

Dennis said, "I know of just such a church and I know the pastor. It's near where you live; I'll contact the pastor on your behalf to introduce you." Dennis, a well-known author and Christian conference speaker, could see Laura's face light up with the prospect of finding a church home. Dennis knew this church and its pastor and thought this was a place where Laura could find the love and support she needed. Dennis was also aware of the importance of his recommendation on another level. Laura had never attended church but she was now ready to reach out and find the acceptance and love she needed so very much.

On the very next Sunday morning, Laura went to the church that Dennis recommended, excited about the prospects of finding a church where she could begin to work through a lifetime of hurts. This was a big day. She walked into the small older church building. Some ladies quickly welcomed her, "Hello!" "Welcome!" "Nice to meet you!" "Would you like to give us your address and phone number for our newcomer book so we can get to know you better?" Laura stayed for a few minutes in the well-worn lobby making small talk with the ladies, and then excused herself. She walked inside to where the pastor would speak and found a seat midway down on the right.

Laura looked around. She could see the church fixtures had seen years of first-timers walking in as she did. She was a little uncomfortable and unsure of herself this first time in church. The ladies who had talked to her in the lobby walked inside also, sitting on both sides of Laura to make her feel at ease and welcome. "Ahhh," Laura breathed a sigh of relief as their kindness filled her with an unfamiliar feeling of acceptance and warmth.

Laura enjoyed the service. When it was over, not feeling sociable and still a little awkward and uncomfortable, Laura made a quick exit to her car and drove home. Later in the afternoon, Laura looked out her front window and noticed a car with the lights on parking near her front door. The car door opened and it was the senior pastor. Laura was blown away by this special visit. "Wow, amazing! What a special church and pastor! The pastor is coming to visit me on my first day!" Laura smiled wide, her spirits lifted high at the thought. After all, it was her first time in the little church and Dr. Dennis Guernsey had recommended it. Very excited, Laura walked toward the front door to open it. The senior pastor was now knocking on the front door. Laura quickly opened the door and expectantly said; "Hello, Pastor, come on in."

But Laura noticed this pastor was not smiling as he briskly entered her home. Laura could feel the fresh air being sucked out of the room, replaced by rising tension before he even said a word. Awkwardness filled the moment as Laura, now silent, waited for him to speak. The pastor did not exchange pleasantries or sit down. He simply stood silently just a step or two inside Laura's living room. Laura was now quite puzzled and thought, "Why is he here?" Finally after much hesitation, he spoke. "Laura, we don't want your kind in our church." Laura quickly responded with her own question for him (I love this): "What kind do you want?"

That is a great question to ask any pastor, but especially one who is spouting his own ideas about who should not be sitting in his church. Is it really "his" church? I think not.

I was shocked when I learned of Laura's first church experience. In fact, I was blown away. I serve as the director of care ministries in a large Southern California church and I deal with people all day long but would never ever tell anyone, especially a curvaceous lady, "We do not want your kind in our church."

Sharing this story is important. Church leadership and people who attend church need to learn and be challenged by what Laura's story brings to us all. People are starving for the love of Jesus. Why would any pastor reject a person who was actively seeking such love? Let's carefully unwrap and unfold Laura's story in detail to discover the answer.

Chapter 2

The Call for Help

In serving Jesus Christ do you think we should be the ones to make the choice of who to reject or who to bring to Christ? Or, do you think Christ will do the selecting and bring to us the ones he wants us to lead back to him? I think sometimes we forget we are servants to our Lord. When we remember whom we serve, we know we are called to offer Christ's salvation to everyone, even the ones we do not like much. Perhaps at one time we were not so lovable ourselves.

Remember Laura went to this church for two reasons: one, it was near her home; and two, because Laura's therapist, Fuller Seminary PhD. Dennis Guernsey had called the church's senior pastor whom he had known for some time to let him know Laura needed a church home and she would be attending. Perhaps Dennis did disclose too many personal details about Laura's past to the pastor and that caused him to reject her. Laura was in her early forties, about 5'6" and about 135 pounds with a nice figure. She was seeking the Lord but was rejected by the pastor.

What made her so bad anyway? Laura was not drunk, disruptive, abusive, or unkind in any way, although her life story was very messy. Some of the ladies who had learned of Laura's story from the senior pastor's wife had shown Laura great compassion that Sunday she attended, but none of that compassion came from the senior pastor later that same afternoon as he stood in her living room.

All churches encounter strange, unusual people who challenge us. For example, just recently the church receptionist called me to the lobby because a man wanted counseling and said he could not wait for an appointment with our staff Ph.D.

So down the stairs I went, not knowing what to expect. I walked up, introduced myself and after a few words back and forth with him I felt alarm bells going off. His overall vibe was "scary."

He explained that every TV station in the United States was monitoring his every move—spy cameras in his house, car, and everywhere he went. "And why would they do that?" I asked. "Because I slapped my ex-wife and killed a cat with a shovel. Does that scare you?" I thought to myself, "It's starting to…" and I was pleased to see that he did not have a shovel with him. "How long ago did these events take place?" I asked. "Eight years ago." Everything he was telling me took place eight years ago.

I asked "Have you ever accepted Jesus Christ as your Lord and Savior?" He promptly responded emphatically, "NO! I don't believe in that stuff."

"Why then did you come to a church for help?"

"Because I needed someone that would listen to me."

"Okay, I'm here for you and I will listen." I also thought, "But I'll lead him outside the building in case he turns dangerous."

As we talked, it took me several attempts to guide him to the present, the reality of the moment. "You understand that this moment we are in is not eight years ago, right?"

He paused, looked away for a time as if he were stunned; then he smiled, took a deep breath, and said, "Yeah, you're right; that is not now."

He asked me, "Do you think I'm a bad person?" I said, "No, but you did do some bad things eight years ago." I explained, "Good people sometimes do bad things, and the Lord went to the cross so we would be forgiven and redeemed for them." Then I asked, "Can I pray for you?" He did not say no quickly enough, so I placed my hands on his shoulders and prayed. The words that came were not mine; the Lord carefully provided all the words for the prayer. When I finished praying, I hugged him, and away he went with a smile. Sometimes the best and only caring we can offer is found in prayer. I pray this was the case with this man.

The challenging situations I face in caring for all who attend my church are wide-ranging from severe psychiatric cases to folks who are just disruptive. People in the midst of major life struggles truly need someone to listen, comfort, and pray with them. They can challenge us. It's a challenge for us as Christians to remember that everyone is redeemable and everyone has a testimony we can learn from, as we can see from the cast of characters from the Bible.

To see if we should reject all such people as if they would never be fit to sit in a church or to serve God, we should look at the people in Scripture who God used to serve him:

Jeremiah .... was depressed and suicidal
John the Baptist .... was a loud mouth
Hosea's wife .... was a prostitute
John .... was self-righteous
Peter .... was afraid to die
Jonah .... ran from God
Paul .... was a murderer
Noah.. got drunk
Martha .... was a worrywart
Mary.. was lazy

You get the idea. We need to be sure we do not become too self-righteous ourselves, thinking we have permission to reject people just because we don't like them. It's important to evaluate their openness to personal transformation on an ongoing basis as the Lord leads them down that path.

What was Laura's story? Laura's troubles began at a very young age during the 1940s when psychology was not a household word. She would often withdraw into silence to repress her feelings, not knowing how to express the hurts she had suffered from trusted loved ones. Grandma had done things that twisted Laura's thoughts. Uncle Fred had fondled her repeatedly for years. Mom and Dad's form of discipline was common among households in the 1940s but became excessive in her case. So, with no place to turn, Laura's deep unresolved hurts turned into something more serious—psychological issues that continued into her teen years and into adulthood.

Seriously plagued by mental torment, Laura turned to a radical surgical procedure that was touted to be the "cure." But tragically, she underwent a surgery that was completely unnecessary for resolving her mental distress and heaped on her even more devastation. Laura found herself broken, alone, seemingly beyond any hope of help.

The challenge for any church when faced with broken, messy people is to look into their eyes, as if looking at Jesus Christ himself, understanding that He might have sent this person special delivery, just for you. But we sometimes look at such folks only as if their primary purpose is to disrupt our daily tasks, yet that is hardly a reason to reject them.

Laura's difficult journey started during childhood, but by the age of 42, Laura was suffering with more than the usual emotional and financial struggles. She was badly broken, in deep emotional pain and severe financial distress. She was contemplating taking her own life, to the extent of actually planning the suicide. She was exhausted and wanted to end it all. The struggle which had begun in her teens had gone on too long. In her distress Laura contacted her previous therapist, Dr. Guernsey. During the office visit, he became alarmed by the depth of Laura's depression and the intensity of her talk about suicide.

Dr. Guernsey knew Laura could not be alone and needed to be with people. Dennis thought a family environment would be best. Knowing that being alone would be risky for her, Dennis asked Laura, "Would you be willing to move into a home with a family?" She responded, "Yes." Dennis started making calls to longtime friends to find a family that would care for Laura. Dr. Guernsey felt he needed to disclose to prospective families all the history of Laura's troubled life. After hearing the details, most answered "No" to his request. They did not want a very depressed, troubled Laura in their home.

Absolutely no one could accurately diagnose Laura's psychological problems; all the psychologists were puzzled. All anyone knew was she had been troubled and tormented from her early childhood, but the diagnosis was undetermined. She had wild and frequent swings from feeling that she was "living the dream life" thinking that the radical treatment procedure had cured her deep psychological issues, to feeling suicidal.

After several calls Dennis found a pastor he had known from the old days at Dallas Theological Seminary, his old friend Roy, who was willing to consider including Laura in his family. Roy was married with two children in high school. Roy had earned his Ph.D. in cross-cultural psychology and a master's degree in theology.

Roy's wife, Bonita, was a longtime school teacher with a gift of love for people who needed help. Roy and Bonita were a good choice, given their love for helping people. Roy was a solid guy, with a great family.

Dennis had a friend who owned the Rocky Mountain Chocolate Factory store in San Francisco at the Embarcadero Center. Dennis knew he could get Laura a job there, and she was all for it. Dennis also wanted Laura to be able to pay her way and not just live off the generosity of the Thompson family.

Roy, his wife Bonita, and their children Kristina and Jon prepared their home for Laura. Laura would be loved even when she was not so lovable. Everyone in the family placed their trust and faith in Christ. They knew Christ would show them the way even though they did not know where it would take them. Laura and the family quickly bonded, just sitting and talking into the late evening hours, night after night, talking and laughing. They referred to this time as having "deep philosophical discussions."

Night after night in bed alone, Laura cried until her pillow was wet, mourning her life and how completely it was messed up, seemingly beyond any hope of repair. Questions and doubts haunted her, and the biggest question was: "Can my messed-up life ever amount to anything good?

Chapter 3

The Thompson Family

I opened the door and there before us was a woman in a red sweater fit snugly over her well-endowed figure with bright red lipstick and fingernails and shoulder-length hair. "You must be Laura!" I said, inviting her in. Thus began a journey that turned "a few days" into nine months and nine months into twenty plus years of relationship.

We had no precedent for this situation in other relationships, nor did we find any specific Scripture to act as a road map through this minefield. We did know that we had a responsibility to love her. About this, Scriptures were clear.

—Dr. Roy Thompson

Roy realized that Laura's situation did not fit within any world he had known. She was an alcoholic who struggled with psychological issues and her very identity. She was very bright, but had lost touch with reality. Everything she had worked for before was gone, completely eradicated by the consequences of her bad choices.

What were those choices? The most shocking was Laura's decision prior to knowing the Thompsons to undergo a radical treatment—a radical surgery the doctors said would cure her, but instead made everything worse. Laura always hated the fact she was born a male. Being male seemed to be the cause of all her confusion and pain; so after much counseling and soul-searching, she underwent gender change surgery. In her forties she became "Laura."

The sexual reassignment surgery made Laura a surgical woman using the same body that originally was male. Laura altered her appearance to match her new surgical gender. But the Lord did not give up on her as she underwent numerous cosmetic procedures in an all-out effort to give her a real chance at successfully passing as, and living as, a woman. Laura changed her legal identity by exchanging her male driver's license for a female driver's license and successfully petitioned the courts to change her birth certificate to female, with her new female name.

But Laura was exhausted and confused from an internal conflict that had lasted more than 35 years. She had been in therapy off and on for 15 years, and obviously still needed help. Starting over with the Thompson family brought her a feeling of great hope that their stable family environment would bring her freedom from her unsettled thoughts. She stood at the proverbial crossroads of her life standing on the doorstep of a home where she would be loved as part of a family.

In addition to Roy and Bonita and their children Kristina and Jon, the Thompson family had one more member: "Granny," Roy's mother, a very proper high-society Texas woman who loved the Lord. Granny's confrontational nature made teenager Kristina seems withdrawn by comparison.

Laura remembers trying to impress Granny one evening by sharing her career experience. Laura told Granny how she had worked on the Apollo space mission project as an associate design engineer, and about the high level career she had had in the auto industry with Honda, both as national port operations manager and as one of the small team who had secretly developed the new Acura division. Laura knew that would impress the old gal. When Laura was finished crowing about all her career accomplishments, Granny responded by saying, "Well, if you're so smart, why did you do something so stupid?" Granny blew the wind completely out of Laura's sails. Laura was breathless and could not speak because she had no answer. The Lord was using this old lady to get Laura's attention and Laura was slowly getting the message, or was she?

Laura started her new job during the summer of 1985, commuting via bus, the BART rail system and a short walk to the Rocky Mountain Chocolate Factory store in San Francisco. Laura was looking for a fresh start, while she dealt with her "stuff." And now she was generating her own financial support from working.

After a few months of living with the Thompson family, surrounded by loving people whose only interest was her restoration, attending church on a regular basis, not drinking, and working at the Rocky Mountain Chocolate Factory, Laura felt she was ready to go off on her own and get an apartment. She found one near the Thompsons'.

All those months spent with the Thompson family had provided Laura with a powerful "model" of healthy people and she wanted to be healthy. It was becoming clear to her that God created her as a man. Laura was able to understand that the identity of Laura was the result of an unresolved psychological disorder, and that Laura was not a real person. Laura knew what she would do. She decided to face the truth and return to living life in her birth gender and stop the lie of living as a surgical woman.

So Laura told Roy she wanted to quit her job as Laura at the Rocky Mountain Chocolate Factory store in San Francisco and get a job as a man, and start over trying to restore his male identity and broken life. His middle name is James; and to protect his identity, we will just call him "Jim."

Roy had a friend named Ed who owned a business in Sunnyvale, about 40 minutes from Roy's. Roy called Ed and asked if he could find a place for Jim to work in his big auto-motive body shop. Ed, Roy, and Jim had lunch a few days later; and Ed said he would give Jim a chance and work him into the swing of things as a male. Jim liked Ed and thought he was a real cool guy.

Jim was now working as a male in an automotive body shop with a boss who would do all he could to help Jim shed the identity of Laura. But living life as a male was now a constant, confusing contradiction: surgical female, living and acting as a male. Returning to his male birth gender was far more difficult than anyone could have imagined. Unfortunately, in an effort to cope, Jim went back to his old friend alcohol to cope with the confusion. Jim had been sober several months, but it was all about to unravel as Jim began drinking excessively.

One morning, after drinking late the previous night, Jim went to work where Ed smelled the alcohol on his breath. Jim noticed the look in Ed's eyes and the expression on his face—a combination of disappointment and disgust. Furious, Ed wanted Jim out of his body shop. He walked Jim to his car, opened the door, and said, "You're fired." Jim responded by saying, "Is that the way you deal with difficult issues; just kick them out of your life?" It struck a cord with Ed, and he relented, "Come back tomorrow, but only if you do not smell of alcohol."

Ed immediately alerted his friend Roy. Roy was waiting for Jim when he arrived home to his apartment. Jim explained to Roy he wanted to return again to his identity as Laura. Being Jim was just too difficult.

This would be the beginning of a protracted, pitiful see-saw pattern, back and forth between two genders and the identities of Laura and Jim. Much like an addict uses their addiction to escape pain and reality, living as Laura gave Jim a temporary escape from the pain of reality. But like the addict, the shame created difficulties for his psyche. The shame of having a body that was surgically altered to look like a female and trying to live life as a male was all too much. Jim switched to Laura, then back to Jim, when the pain of living as one pushed him to try life as the other. Roy Thompson remembers:

Laura talked to therapist after therapist, wanting to discover a way out of the confusion. More diagnoses came: severe depression, post traumatic stress disorder, schizophrenia, gender identity disorder. Everyone had an opinion. We researched them all. None of them quite fit. None of these could explain the flip-flopping we were witnessing. We were confused. Jim/Laura was confused.

What a tailspin at times we all experienced. Dissatisfied and restless, Laura again questioned her identity and Jim reappeared.

Over a period of several years he went from Jim to Laura, Laura to Jim and back again. It was not unusual. There were times we felt that Laura was it, finally permanent. Then Jim would reappear. We could not imagine the confusion and trauma that greeted this psyche every morning.

—Dr. Roy Thompson

To Roy's credit, when Jim said he wanted to be Laura again, Roy said, "Stay home and don't drink. I'll be back in a few hours." In the meantime, Roy went looking for and found a therapist at the Stanford University campus whose career was devoted to working with transsexuals and transvestites who, like Jim, were suffering from complete dislike of their birth gender. Roy arranged for Laura to start having regular sessions with her. Roy was hopeful the therapist could help control the swings Jim/Laura was having back and forth with gender identity.

The stern and no-nonsense therapist was a member of the Board of the International Gender Dysphoria Association, a group that advocated sex change surgery and living life as a transgender as appropriate treatment for the disorder. She was personal friends with Paul Walker, the Ph.D. who originally approved Laura for surgery. The therapist took time during the first few sessions to learn Jim's history: Jim's childhood problems, the sense of being trapped in a man's body, and so forth.

"Jim, your symptoms and history are typical of gender dysphoria. And I will tell you this: yours is the worst case of gender identity confusion I've ever seen. Having the surgery was the proper treatment. Know that a lot of people who go through the surgery have difficulty at first adjusting. In my opinion, you probably haven't given life as Laura enough time."

But Jim knew in his heart that a surgical woman was not a real woman no matter how much he felt like one. Jim also knew the Lord was telling him the truth: he was a man and the surgery could not change that.

But the therapist was confident the surgery was the proper treatment for this disorder. So instead of helping Jim to cope, the therapy was making coping even more difficult. Jim was in a battle for his life, as he was being torn between two genders. Laura's influence was growing; she was becoming more powerful than Jim, and he found himself unable to stop Laura. Living as either gender was becoming more uncomfortable and provided no psychological rest, not as Jim or Laura. Jim was in tremendous psychological pain. Adding to his pain was seeing how his obvious battle over his gender was troubling to everyone who cared about him.

If the surgery was the "proper treatment" why was it so difficult for either Jim or Laura to become free of all the twists and turns and switching of genders back and forth?

At home late in the evening, the emotional and psychological pain was so intense Jim would stand in his living room bent over at the waist with both hands firmly placed on his knees for support, and weep and groan with such agony he felt as if his body would explode.

The way out of that pain was to drink—alcohol did provide the numbing effect Jim needed. Unable to cope, Jim changed into Laura again.

Laura decided she would go out drinking for the evening. Deeply confused about the surgery and her gender, she walked toward the biker bars only two blocks from her apartment for that drink, to kill all that pain, at least for the night. After putting back several, no make that many, mind-numbing drinks, Laura thought she had the only answer out of all this confusion. A few blocks away was a local fast-food joint. Walking around to the rear of the building and climbing up a ladder to the rooftop, Laura stood on the edge looking down at a gathering crowd and yelled, "I'm going to commit suicide!" Someone called the local police who came quickly to arrest Laura for being drunk in public.

They took her to the Santa Rita Jail and placed her in a holding cell, a very small holding cell, to sober up. Some hours later Laura was released, and faced a very long walk back to her apartment. In comparison to jail, the apartment was a luxury hotel room.

Either way, as Jim or Laura, she/he was completely unable to cope with life. Living alone with her twisted thoughts was not helping. Was this the end? Jim/Laura was completely filled with shame, in large part because she/he turned to alcohol as the savior for a torn-up life and not to Jesus Christ.

When Roy learned from Laura that she was arrested, he was concerned, and like everyone else, completely out of ideas. He suggested continuing the sessions at Stanford with the transgender specialist. When Ed heard about Jim's episode of drinking and subsequent arrest, he knew Jim needed much more than a job at this point. Ed and his wife

Kathy truly wanted to do anything they could to help, but they were at a loss.

At the sentencing hearing for her public drunkenness violation, the judge gave Laura the following options: go into a recovery treatment facility within three weeks and have the charge expunged from her record, or go to jail for the misdemeanor. The recovery treatment idea was starting to appeal to Laura.

Laura called her transgender therapist to tell her what the judge had offered her ending with the comment: "I'm ready to take the recovery treatment option, if you can find one for me." But Laura showed up for her scheduled appointment slightly intoxicated. Angered, the therapist said; "I have no use for a client coming in here drunk. There is nothing that you can say that I want to hear. You will sit there in that chair, in total silence, for the full length of your session." Shame-faced, Laura complied. The therapist completely ignored Laura as she worked to complete some paperwork.

At the end of the very silent, very uncomfortable forty-five minute period, the therapist slid a paper across her desk toward Laura. On that paper were the phone numbers of three recovery treatment facilities in the local area.

Motivated by the judge's ultimatum to go into a treatment facility, Laura made the call and went for an interview with the manager of the recovery house. She saw the room and the bed that was waiting for her. First, Laura was required to go to a 48-hour detox facility starting that very night or else they would not hold the bed for her. This was a $3500 a month facility, but they held two beds for people who could not pay. That was Laura's case.

Laura drove back to her apartment and called Roy. "I'm going into a woman's recovery home for at least ninety days. Would you help me to vacate the apartment?" With Roy's help, Laura disposed of a few things in the trash and prepared a bag of clothes to take with her to the 48-hour detox. On the way to detox she drove a little out of the way to the body shop and thanked Ed and his wife for truly pouring their hearts out and trying so hard. Loving on Laura even when she was Jim—they were just great people. Laura apologized for any difficulty she had caused. Ed was pleased that she was going "full-bore" for recovery.

With the address of the detox facility in her hand, and evening closing in on the day, Laura drove to a Denny's restaurant near the detox facility. She went into the Denny's with the full intention of going to the bar in the back part of the restaurant, wanting to make sure she had something to detox from. Once in the bar, as she had done for so many years time and time again, Laura planted her butt firmly on the first bar stool. For over twenty-four years this was her pattern: get rip-roaringly drunk and as stupid as a wooden stick. Here she was sitting on a bar stool once again, wondering: "What is different? Could this be the last time?"

Laura took a couple of sips of her red wine. This time, the weight of shame came over her in a way that she had never experienced. So much shame; Laura could not take another sip. She was painfully aware of all the years, all of the wasted time sitting in a bar. The tears slowly welled up in her eyes; she was done. Reality hit her. Everything was gone: marriage, family, career, identity; it was all a big fat mess.

She was well aware that she was now on the scrapheap of humanity, a thrown-away life, destroyed by bad choices. Alcohol, drugs, and surgery had rendered Laura useless to anyone. The identity of Jim had failed miserably as a man, husband, and father. The single issue Jim says hurts more than all the other stuff piled together, that he regrets the most, and that is so difficult to emotionally get through is how he failed his great kids. No child should ever be forced to face the shame of such a troubling issue with their father.

Laura paid for the wine and drove to the detox facility: an unmarked cinderblock building painted no particular color, with steel doors, bars on the windows, and a narrow driveway for parking in the rear. The building resembled a solitary confinement blockade from a horror movie. Laura parked the car and walked around to the front door. It was locked, so she knocked. A very large African-American woman opened the door and said, "We have been waiting for you." Laura introduced herself, "I'm Laura and I'm scared," and started crying.

The fee for detox was twenty dollars a day. Laura paid the two-day fee and cried her heart out as if she were walking to the gallows, as if it were a lynching. Laura did not want to be there. The place was full of bums, prostitutes, and court-ordered stays. "Why do I need to be here?" she thought, but she knew she was just like them. At least she found comfort in knowing that she had a bed ready for her in a recovery house. Tomorrow, May 2, 1986, would be her first day sober.

After the 48 hours in detox, Laura went to the recovery house where she stayed for almost four months. She was introduced as Laura Jensen. No one knew she was a trans-sexual; she was just one of the girls. Laura started the process to restore her broken torn-up life. For four months, Laura went to at least one AA meeting per day, often two per day, along with required classes in the recovery home, and daily individual and group therapy sessions.

Laura shared a bedroom and bath with two other women in what was a pleasant home, and all 14 women gathered around a big table and ate all three meals a day together. The women in this recovery home were allowed to go off the property alone. Two or more together was a mandatory requirement. Laura could have visitors, but no one came to visit Laura except for the transgender therapist. It felt good to see her. The others were just not sure about Laura. Some were, no doubt, standing on the sidelines, waiting for the next flip-flop to Jim or perhaps even fearful of another relapse that would spell the end.

During Laura's four months in the recovery home, she focused solely on alcohol recovery. After successfully completing the program, Laura was out on her own. This time she would not live at the Thompsons' but instead she looked for a place to live close to the outpatient treatment program.

Laura wanted to get back to church. "I want the Lord to start working in my life," she thought. She sought out a church in the local area. In stark and amazing contrast to Laura's first encounter in a church, her next led her to the very feet of God. Jeff was senior pastor. He did not reject Laura at all. He was like a football head coach and inspired his church leadership team to care about Laura.

Jeff set up a prayer team just for Laura. The prayer team consisted of 25 to 30 people from this rather small church who prayed for her regularly. They even had Laura prepare a prayer letter that could be sent to all the prayer team members, so they would know the issues she was facing on a regular basis.

Jeff, along with staff members Pat and Dixie, included Laura in everything, always encouraging her to visit or call the senior pastor whenever she needed to talk or needed anything at all; she only needed to call.

So was this a new start or one more failure in a long line of failures?

Chapter 4

The Biblical View

As I learned about Laura, Jeff and all the others, I knew this incredible story needed to be told. It could inspire those who were normally reluctant to help "scary" people to learn from Jeff's style of pastoring and consider the possibilities when a church truly expresses the love of Jesus, and lives it out on a daily basis.

Jeff was a visionary and his staff was amazing in their support for Laura. It was as if they just completely trusted the Lord to transform Laura's life, when others before had just looked at Laura and said, "Broken beyond repair."

I was definitely uncertain and nervous when Laura walked into my office. My friend, Roy Thompson, had called and explained her story. I remembered being shocked as I listened to Roy, but then struck by the thought of God's power transforming a person in that situation.

After a few minutes of talking, it became apparent that Laura was more nervous than I. While her story was terribly painful, it dawned on me that from her past experience with other pastors and churches, she expected to be judged and rejected.

I determined to encourage her toward the Lord and Scripture no matter what she had to say. Regardless of her experience and choices, she wasn't too much for the Lord to handle. I also felt strongly that I had little to offer Laura. I told her that I had no experience with her situation. Many of the battles she fought and the choices she faced I had never even thought about, let alone encountered. Frankly, I told her, I was afraid that I would do damage to her with any counsel I could come up with. I simply did not know what to say to her.

Laura's answer was, "No one knows what to do with me or say to me. So don't sweat it." One thread through Jim's (then Laura's) life that never changed regardless of the wardrobe was a tremendous sense of humor. Laura was frank, animated and engaging.

Since it was also apparent she was repentant and broken before the Lord and willing to do whatever she needed to honor Him, I could see no choice but to be available to her.

So began one of the most important and significant relationships in my life. As it was cemented through countless meetings over a number of years, I had found a great friend. Jim/Laura turned out to be a tremendous source of encouragement and model of obedience in the middle of tremendous pain. Watching the miraculous growth from Laura to Jim became my greatest source of confidence that God's power still worked today.

From day one of our relationship, Laura (then Jim) was a great friend, a fellow-soldier in the faith. Walking together through the pain, we cried, trusted and laughed as God led us through this journey. I can say without hesitation that having Jim in my life has been a tremendous gift.

—Pastor Jeff Farrar

The Lord, using His power, placed Laura on yet another front door step, this time at a church with a senior pastor named Jeff. As only the Lord can do, He gathered all of His players, the ones He wanted in Laura's life at this very time. I can see the Lord's presence starting to prepare the way for Laura's restoration.

Even as messed up as her life was, being a scary person, a transsexual, Laura was reaching out to the church and she wanted to walk with the Lord. Pastor Jeff was a friend of Roy Thompson's. Jeff was also a friend and high school classmate of Ed, the body shop guy and Jim's previous boss. Laura knew with absolute certainty that the Lord had placed her at this church with this part of the family of Christ, with a pastor who truly had a heart and desire to reach out to scary and unlovable people.

Laura would not get the response "we do not want your kind in our church" here. Pastor Jeff told Laura that the Lord was there for whoever she was. No matter what, the Lord loved her. Jeff did not know if the Lord would heal all the scars and past hurts. But when Jeff spoke to Laura, Jeff used words of hope, love, and encouragement—all words which, like seeds, took root in Laura's heart.

Laura needed a place to stay, since Roy lived on the other side of the San Francisco Bay. She needed to stay close to her recovery program. Living alone would be emotionally risky in early recovery and was not financially possible for her.

Someone from Jeff's church knew a lady named Cathy who was looking for a female roommate. Laura interviewed with her to rent one of the three bedrooms in her apartment, but skipped over the part about being a transsexual. Ignorant of this "little" detail, Cathy agreed to rent Laura the room. As it turned out, the Lord was using His people again. Roy Thompson knew Cathy from a church they had both attended some years earlier. When Laura told Roy she was moving in with Cathy, he asked her if she had shared her wild recovery history with Cathy, or the transsexual part. Laura said, "No."

Roy was not pleased by the deception. Later that week, Laura was at work in her new job in the lingerie section of a local department store—a transsexual in lingerie, that's a wild thing. Laura looked up from the register while ringing up a sale. She saw Cathy walking toward her at about 80 miles per hour—anyway a very fast pace—with fire in her eyes. When Cathy was face-to-face with Laura, she confronted her with what Roy had told her. "You were once a man!" she exclaimed. In the best way Laura knew how, very gently, and with a sincere heartfelt apology, Laura asked for forgiveness for upsetting her. Laura apologized, "Cathy, I'm so sorry. Will you please forgive me?" Cathy hugged Laura and said, "I forgive you, and I want to know how I can help you."

What Laura came to learn about Cathy was that she had a deep commitment to the Lord and profound compassion for people. Cathy told Laura that her strange history did not change her willingness to rent her the room or have her living in her home. The bedroom was not yet available, so Cathy offered Laura the use of the living room couch temporarily. Without hesitation, Laura said, "Yes, that would be great." After about two weeks, the room became available and Laura had a room and great support in Cathy.

Back at church, Pastor Jeff was undaunted by Laura's history as a transsexual or her alcoholism. He had enlisted his staff and the church elders to welcome Laura. The contrast of the welcome at Jeff's church to her rejection at the previous church is striking to me. To me, Jeff's church is a church truly serving and trusting the Lord all the way. His church took the next step to offer Laura support with both finances and prayer.

Laura was especially amazed at two women on Jeff's staff that loved her more than Laura could love herself: Dixie Gilbert, Jeff's right hand at church, and Pat Portman, the central hub of all that happened in and around the church. Pat and Dixie encouraged Laura to write to the prayer team on a regular basis to keep her needs and recovery process before them. The identities of the members of the prayer team were kept from Laura. All communication went through Dixie and Pat to the 30 or so people who pledged their support through money, prayer and love, no matter how long it took.

Laura's letter became known as "the prayer letter." With full transparency Laura shared her most intimate struggles and battles, no matter how bizarre, uncomfortable, or un-Christ-like they may be, so that the prayer team could pray very specifically for healing over those areas.

In my view, speaking as someone who works as a care director in a church, this approach to a scary person is a textbook example of biblical principles being lived out in real life, with no judgment and no fear, just giving it all to the Lord, because the problem is a God-size problem. This was the way to bring the power and grace of Jesus Christ into Laura's life. How many senior pastors and church staff members would take such seemingly risky steps for an alcoholic transsexual like Laura?

Later, in telling her story, Laura said writing the prayer letter was not just a catharsis, but a turning point for her! Finally, she felt deeply loved by each and every person because they put love into action. Now, instead of Laura fleeing into alcohol for some escape or relief, she had safe people to share with and explore the hidden areas that had haunted and tormented her all her life. Having so many people truly interested in her welfare and healing was giving her the motivation and desire to take the necessary steps to allow restoration into her life. Jeff's idea for the prayer letter was brilliant and effective in starting the healing and recovery of Laura's life. God answered the prayers of His saints.

Laura was developing her new relationship with Jesus and was now working a rigorous 12-step program. And the relationships she was developing with Jeff, his staff, and the church family were providing this safe place to open up and share the deep, shameful stuff. Laura's prayer letters were providing unvarnished accounts of her weekly battles and successes. The "Jeff church" used the Lord's tools of unconditional love and prayer to bring change to Laura's broken life. Jeff delights in the process that forges new trophies for Christ, especially in cases where others would have turned their backs and said, "You are too messy."

Chapter 5

Accountability

J eff had a special and unique understanding of just how to keep Laura's eyes on the Lord, without compromising biblical truths. That was what Laura wanted and needed— the truth.

Jeff recalls his thoughts and how he felt the Lord was leading him—

At the end of our first meeting, Laura asked if I would be willing to regularly meet with her. I was acutely aware of how far over my head I was. I knew she wasn't too much for the Lord, just too much for me. I had a sense the Spirit was calling me to encourage her, but I had no idea what that might mean.

Painfully aware of how little I had to offer, I told her two things were necessary for me to be involved with her. First I had to have the freedom to be completely honest with her. I couldn't let my ignorance and inexperience or her fragility keep me from being open with my thoughts, counsel, and questions. She didn't need to agree with me; but without honesty as the basis of our relationship, I couldn't be involved with integrity.

Secondly, my elders needed to know about her. My responsibility and my protection required that I be accountable to them. I asked her to trust me that I would only share as much as was required for them to understand what we were both dealing with. From her past experience, this was very frightening for Laura. Though I assured her that they could be trusted and their prayers were powerful, it put her in a position of great vulnerability. Looking back I can see that this was a much greater act of courage and trust on Laura's part than I realized at the time.

Our sessions together weren't centered on psychological counsel. That important piece was ongoing alongside our meetings. My goal was to encourage her toward the Lord, to move her ahead in:

- *honesty before God in prayer*
- *biblically-based decision making*
- *accountability in her lifestyle decisions*
- *freedom to accept God's grace and tenderness.*

Some Convictions That Compelled Us

Jesus' example obligated us to accept and reach out to Laura.

One day Jesus was hosting a lunch of certain "types" of people–"tax-gatherers and sinners." Mark emphasizes the fact that "there were many of them, and they were following Him" (Mark 2:15, New American Standard Bible). Some religious leaders were scandalized by this and asked the disciples how He could eat and drink with such people. Jesus' response is powerful. He says, "It is not those who are healthy who need a physician, but those who are sick; I did not come to call the righteous, but sinners" (Mark 2:17, NASB).

When I looked around at our church, there weren't many people outside of our comfort zone. Laura came from a horrible, terrifying situation. The fact that she was a challenge was no reason not to engage and serve her.

The issues facing us weren't really about Laura but about what kind of a church we were.

Matthew 25 describes that the Lord judges us based on our treatment of hurting, needy people. The ones accepted are those of whom Jesus says "For I was hungry, and you gave Me something to eat; I was thirsty, and you gave Me drink; I was a stranger, and you invited Me in; naked and you clothed Me; I was sick and you visited Me; I was in prison, and you came to Me" (Matthew 25:35, 36, NASB). It is fascinating that those called to meet His needs never saw Him. Jesus' answer is "that the extent that you did it (or did not do it) to one of these brothers of Mine, even the least of them, you did it (or did not do it) to me" (Matthew 25:40, 45, NASB).

I believe the Spirit was inviting us into a new level of obedience and trust. I had some sense that how we dealt with Laura would determine the type of leaders and the type of church we would be. We had talked (even bragged) about being a community of grace, yet here was a person whose need forced us to either live that out in the midst of uncertainty and trust, or choose safety and pass her by.

Our call was to obey the Lord in ministry and not preserve the status quo or avoid criticism.

Pastors and elders are rightly aware of protecting the church. Yet it is a small step from proper concern for the good of the church to protecting our reputation as leaders and avoiding criticism. It is clear from Jesus' model that His character was defamed due to His commitment to loving needy, even "scary" people. Jesus defends His choices to fellowship with these people and recounts how His enemies tried to use it against Him. "The Son of Man has come eating and drinking; and you say, 'Behold, a gluttonous man, and a drunkard, a friend of tax-gatherers and sinners" (Luke 7:34, NASB). They didn't say these things because Jesus ate too much food and drank too much wine. It was because of those He spent time with and shared meals with.

We were aware that many would just not understand why we would welcome a person like Laura in our church. We discussed the fact that if Laura became visible, some might even leave the church. After thinking this through, our conclusion was that those individuals probably needed to leave the church and find a place that would better suit them. There was much more at stake here than simply keeping attendance numbers up.

Laura was hurting and broken before the Lord, not rebellious or defiant.

This became the determining factor in how we responded to people in need. I often probed Laura and asked the Lord for insight into her heart. There is a world of difference between a broken person and a defiant person. Someone who has failed and is weak and hurting needs to be encouraged, lifted up, gently pointed to the truth, and urged to trust the Lord. A defiant person needs to be exhorted, confronted, and even opposed by the weight of Scripture in the hope of pulling them back to obedience.

While Laura's past choices were, by her own admission, at best foolish and destructive, her longing to honor God in the midst of her pain and willingness to follow the truth were apparent. She wasn't a person defiantly shaking her fist at God claiming she had the right to do whatever she wanted. She was crushed and bowed before God seeking His will in the midst of the mess her life had become. Even when we as a church did not understand her situation, it was her heart that obligated us to engage her in love and support.

As Laura became part of the church, we who knew her past were sometimes faced with tough ethical choices. When would protecting her "secret" compromise us? I don't know that we always made the wisest decisions. There were times we had to face the ones who were kept in the dark for Laura's protection who felt betrayed when they discovered the whole story. In those painful moments, we were compelled to shelter Laura/Jim from even knowing those things were occurring. Deciding to do what we as elders believed was biblically correct certainly didn't exempt us from difficult times and some painful encounters.

— *Pastor Jeff Farrar*

Chapter 6

A Church that Cares

W hat are we in churches going to do with messy people? They do not look like we want them to look, and instinctively, we want to reject them. Because most often we just do not know what to do with them, especially if they are too messy for a hug. Because I'm on staff as the director of care ministries in a large church, I understand the importance of protecting the church attendees from anyone who could be considered a danger to themselves or others. It is easy to move into action when people clearly are combative, abusive, or pose a danger. We need to recognize that messy people are not a threat, combative, or abusive. Instead, they challenge us to show compassion because they do not look "normal."

In Jim Cymbala's book *Fresh Wind, Fresh Fire*, he gives fresh examples of people just waiting to be built into trophies of God. Cymbala writes:

> We never knew who might come to Christ at the Brooklyn Tabernacle. There were junkies, prostitutes, and homosexuals. But lost lawyers, business types, and bus drivers turned to the Lord there, too. We welcomed them all.

There were Latinos, African Americans, Caribbean Americans, whites—you name it. Once people were energized by the Holy Spirit, they began to see other races as God's creation. Instead of railing at homosexuals, we began to weep over them. (p. 33-34)

So many times, the church sets in motion an "us against them" mentality, like the pastor did with Laura when he said, "We do not want your kind in our church." I think churches have done great harm by setting themselves up as a battlefield, not considering the possibilities or how Christ looks at "scary" people. But it need not be that way.

Cymbala tells this story from his experience at the Brooklyn Tabernacle:

Walking down the center aisle, I bumped into an attractive woman in a black dress, with blond, shoulder-length hair, nicely done nails, black stockings, and high heels. "Excuse me, ma'am," I said.

She turned...and in a low voice with a heavy accent replied, "No, that's okay, man."

My heart skipped a beat. That was not a woman after all. But neither was it a sloppy transvestite. This was a knockout of a "woman"—bone-thin, no body hair thanks to hormonal treatment...

His name was Ricardo, known on the street as "Sarah." (p. 76)

Ricardo was a $400 to $600 a night street hustler and spent most of that money on crack cocaine. Ricardo was a homosexual. He had tried to leave the lifestyle but to no avail. Ricardo was attending the Tuesday night prayer meetings, he started to think "this Jesus" could set him free from crack cocaine, maybe even change him into a true man. After about a month, he gave his heart to Jesus. Cymbala writes:

> In the months that followed, Ricardo made great progress in his spiritual life. It took three months to get him straight enough even to be accepted in a drug rehabilitation program. Nevertheless, his commitment to follow Christ was solid. The old had gone; the new had definitely come.
>
> Ricardo had come from out of pitch blackness and into the light...God does his most stunning work where things seem hopeless. (p. 78)

Ricardo moved to Dallas. One summer Cymbala ran into him. Ricardo looked great, a complete transformation, all man. Ricardo announced to Cymbala he had met a Christian woman named Betty and they were getting married.

Those, my fellow Christians, are the possibilities even with a transvestite homosexual. Your God is big enough. The question is: are you? Jim Cymbala's book is full of such stories.

What would have happened to Ricardo if Cymbala would have told him, "We do not want your kind in our church"? We who serve our Lord and Savior on church staffs across the nation all too often look at some groups as unredeemable because we are uncomfortable with what we see. I think God sees an opportunity to transform a life. We need to share God's vision.

Remember this: if we in the church do not provide a safe place of love to transform the lives of homosexuals, transgenders and others who struggle with all kinds of stuff we do not want to talk about, then we have no business calling ourselves Christ followers. Cymbala got it.

You church-goers can make a difference but only when you touch those who scare you; put your arms around them and tell them, "My job is to love you; it's God's job to change you." That's what Jeff did in his church. Like Cymbala, Jeff trusted the power of prayer, love, and Jesus Christ to transform the lives of the "scary people." Jeff knew his job was to provide the love; God's job was to provide the transformation.

And it all starts with prayer. We need prayer to have the Holy Spirit move us to embrace "scary" people, and the "scary" people need prayer for the Lord to intervene in their lives and to allow the Holy Spirit to provide the transformation. You will never in a million years transform a single life by clubbing someone over the head with your favorite Scripture or telling them they are sinners because you also, my friend, are a sinner, and they will see through your veil of hypocrisy. Get real and love them, because you are one of them.

Chapter 7

Taking Baby Steps

During the stay in the recovery house, Laura was drawn toward God. She was starting to understand God's desire for her life and starting to know the Lord was and had always been there, just waiting for her to embrace Him. The 12-step program talks about a higher power, and Laura knew it was Jesus Christ.

Laura attended Jeff's church on a regular basis, and as time went by, Laura's history did not cause much attention at church anymore. Everyone showed her great respect and desired for her to come to a place of internal rest, whatever that would turn out to be.

Pastor Jeff knew how to have fun and laugh and tell jokes. He had real love in his heart for Jesus Christ, and his gift was showing love for the unlovable. Laura was beginning to understand that God had orchestrated the connections between the people along her journey that ultimately placed her in this very special small church family to be loved in a special way.

The department store where Laura had been working was going out of business. It was only a few blocks from church. Laura's last few weeks at the store were spent in the china department, packing up the crystal giftware and dishes. Laura by now had a solid year of sober living and her recovery process was becoming remarkable, thanks to regular attendance at 12-step meetings, and the accountability that came from writing the weekly prayer letter to the church prayer team. But Laura needed a new job, and thankfully, the state of California had programs to help her find employment—a benefit of having successfully completed a recovery program. The state Department of Rehabilitation assigned a counselor to assist Laura in her job search. Laura's state counselor was very sensitive to her unusual history and the counselor liked working with Laura.

In 1987 tolerance for transsexuals in the workplace was non-existent. Back in the days when Laura was so gung-ho on having the surgery, she had naively never considered how potential employers would react to such an applicant. Completing a job application would require that Laura put both male and female names on the application in order to reveal her employment history. Of course, she hadn't thought about that—but then Laura hadn't considered the crushing impact of any of the consequences of her actions. The only thing driving Laura's decision to have surgery was the single-minded pursuit to stop the internal conflict between male and female. Now four years after the surgery, Jim's incredible ascent up the ladder of success in corporate America was but a memory; an inconvenient truth. Jim's experiences as an associate design engineer on the Apollo space mission and his qualifications as an executive in the car business were useless to Laura in finding employment. Laura was sober and she faced the devastating consequences, in full reality. Now at age 47, Jim's career was washed up. Laura would need to carve out a new start on her own. She could not fall back on Jim's skill and experience.

Applying for a job as Laura Jensen was a demoralizing and frustrating experience—a real minefield. If she entered "Jim" under the section "other names used," she had to explain the change from male to female in the interview, a story so bizarre and shocking in those times that it inevitably led to a highly embarrassing and uncomfortable interview; one which slammed the door shut on any prospect of employment.

Laura's other unappealing alternative was to leave "Jim" off the application, get found out, and be denied employment because she had lied on the application. I think they call this a Catch-22.

For example, Laura agonized over her application with United Airlines, whether to put "Jim" on it or not. After much worrying, she decided to try leaving "Jim" off the application. They turned her down for a minimum wage job cleaning airplanes because they found out she did not place Jim's name on the application, because she was not truthful.

Even though Laura knew she was well-qualified for various state government openings, her applications were denied because she did not disclose she was a transsexual. How ironic—the same state that issued her a new birth certificate declaring that she was a female named Laura Jensen, now claimed "foul" because Laura didn't say she was a transsexual on the application. No more chances here—working for the state was out. Even when Laura's state employment counselor called to pave the way, they said no way.

Laura's state employment counselor had a list of other companies that regularly hired referrals from the Department of Rehabilitation. Laura went to every interview the counselor arranged—more than fifty interviews in all.

Finally, success! Laura was hired. The federal government agency, Federal Deposit Insurance Corporation (FDIC), in San Francisco hired Laura to operate a photocopy machine. Operating photocopy machines at FDIC was no sit-down job. An extraordinary number of bank failures were occurring in the late 1980s, and each one necessitated the copying of thousands of pages. The anxiety of looking for work was over. Laura had a solid job with the federal government.

She rented a cheap, tiny studio apartment in the outer Mission District of San Francisco and moved from Cathy's place.

Laura felt real pumped and re-energized by her job, so much so that she dreamt of reaching another goal, to study to become a drug and alcohol counselor. Laura started taking night and weekend classes at the University of California Santa Cruz extension campus in Cupertino, about forty-five miles south of the city. Laura's goal was to attain an advanced studies certificate, the first step to becoming an alcohol drug counselor to help others recover.

By the end of the year, Laura had finished all the first-year classes offered in Cupertino. She had done pretty well allocating her time among working days at FDIC in the city, school in the evenings, homework on the weekends. Church remained important and she never lost contact with the prayer team. Her recovery program consisted of church on the weekends and AA meetings throughout the week. She said even the driving wasn't too bad: ninety miles roundtrip to school during the week, sixty miles roundtrip to church on the weekend.

But now this balancing act that was Laura's life was about to be stretched to the limit. The second-year classes were only available at the main campus in Santa Cruz, a much longer and more time-consuming commute. What had been ninety miles roundtrip to classes became one hundred and fifty miles several days a week. Laura needed more hours in the day to squeeze in all her commitments. Laura's job at FDIC wasn't available as a night job, so she asked for and received a transfer to the U. S. Postal Service, sorting mail on the 11 p.m. to 6 a.m. shift at the Rincon Annex in San Francisco. Laura moved to San Carlos, about twenty-five miles south of San Francisco, close to church, and "only" fifty miles to school.

In this state of exhaustion due to her work and school schedule, Laura was experiencing a new level of difficulty in the gender battle. Laura battled for internal control; Jim now wanted to return to become the man God had uniquely designed him to be. Inexplicably, Laura became terribly uncomfortable in her skin as Laura. Laura couldn't find peace as Jim tried to push his way back.

The fight for control caused a compulsive, irrational swing, almost without warning, back and forth between being Jim and Laura. Pull off the highway, take off the dress and put on the slacks. Wipe off the lipstick and comb out the hair. Or vice versa, put on the dress and the lipstick and pouf, up goes Laura's hair. The differences between Jim and Laura did not stop at appearance. Jim ate junk food; Laura ate healthy food. Jim had a low voice; Laura spoke in a higher pitched range. Jim's handwriting was completely different than Laura's. Taste in music and opinions on issues were even different at times.

There was a loud argument raging inside the mind, "You aren't a man—you had surgery. You're a woman now. Just go look at your birth certificate. It says Laura. What are you doing dressed as a man?" Or as Laura, the opposite thoughts jeered at her: "It's all a masquerade. How can you be a woman? The surgeon cannot change a gender; he is not God. You were born a man and you are a man."

At school and at work Laura couldn't change from Laura to Jim, so she stayed Laura. But outside of those places, Laura frequently changed back and forth from Laura to Jim. She went to men's AA meetings as Jim and to women's AA meetings as Laura, but avoided the mixed meetings. It was far too confusing for Laura or Jim to deal with.

With the Lord Jesus Christ as His strength, Jim would emerge. Then, overwhelmed by all the devastation he had caused his two children, Jim hid in the identity of Laura in order to escape from the pain of the shame. But now that was not working. The battle and pain were growing intense.

Laura realized that if she ever hoped to achieve recovery from the psyche battle, the key would be long-term sobriety. It became Laura's mantra: "Stay sober—no matter what—stay sober." The prayer letters that she prepared weekly for the support team were the key to remaining accountable in her sobriety and in working through the shame of her past.

The group at church continued to assist Laura in support of her recovery and the restoration of Jim. They knew it was all in God's hands. Laura stayed connected with those whose support was essential: Roy and his family, Pastor Jeff and the church, and the two Christian psychologists with whom she had regular sessions.

When Laura was having trouble coping, it hurt her supporters all the more. Laura could not find the words to adequately express to others what was happening in her psyche. The explanations came across as just a bunch of twisted thinking, and it was.

Laura's friends witnessed and experienced the struggle occurring between Laura and Jim. Changing from Laura to Jim could occur within moments. Each had very different opinions, different tastes in food, different voice pitch, and different styles of clothing, each struggling to exert control over the other. The inconsistency between the two personalities was mind-blowing. Frustration ran high and some church members said that Laura was addicted to sex or pornography, but they were wrong. She didn't suffer from those issues at all.

Miraculously, Laura did persevere in her studies and attained her advanced certificate in drug and alcohol studies at the end of two years, in 1989. Laura was three years sober, forty-nine years old, and ready to use her hard-earned training and skills. Once again the switch from Laura to Jim was unfolding. With the start of a new career, Laura felt like it was a good time to look for a job as Jim, a man.

By February of 1990, with Roy Thompson's help, Laura—now back to Jim—became a full-fledged drug and alcohol counselor at CityTeam Ministries in San Jose. Jim was granted a one-year contract at their rehab center, working four days a week with clients. Jim facilitated group counseling and one-on-one counseling, taught classes on recovery, and worked with the state Department of Rehabilitation to help people who completed the one-year recovery program to find jobs. What an amazing twist—now Jim was helping others.

Roy Thompson also worked at CityTeam. Jim did not want to live alone and asked if he could move back in with the Thompson family and they agreed. Jim's contract at CityTeam was for four days a week. This provided Jim an opportunity to spend three days of each week elsewhere. Jim had his eye on a place, the beautiful, sleepy little gold rush town of Murphys in the foothills of the Sierra Nevada mountains, about a two-and-a-half hour drive from the Thompsons' Pleasanton home.

When Laura first started attending recovery meetings during her time at the recovery house, one of the people she got to know was Tommy O. This guy was at almost every meeting Laura attended; he was an old timer. Laura had been to Tommy's home in Murphys several times as part of a large group and Tommy invited Laura to spend three days a week with his family in Murphys. The small-town Murphys lifestyle was so appealing that Laura rented a tiny house next to Tommy O's to live in three days each week.

You're probably wondering like I did: Why didn't Jim just be Jim everywhere? Why maintain two identities: Laura in Murphys and Jim at CityTeam? As Jim explained to me, Laura was very territorial. If Laura was the persona who first came to know the person, it felt too difficult or even impossible for her to bring "Jim" into the relationship. Laura was the one who originally met Tommy O. when she was in the female recovery house, so she felt compelled to be Laura in Murphys. In the strange world that was Jim/Laura's psyche, it made sense.

When a new coffee shop opened on Main Street, Laura showed up as the second customer and quickly became friends with the young couple who owned it. They were fun and their coffee shop became a new hangout for the old town. Their entire family—children and parents alike—adopted Laura as their own. They became significant links in a well-spring of love and friendship that helped to keep Laura on the path of recovery.

This living arrangement was a great combination for Jim/Laura's recovery from alcohol. Four days a week, Jim worked as a counselor in the CityTeam Christian recovery program in San Jose, with Bible study and 12-step studies. Three days a week, Laura lived in Murphys next to her sponsor who had over twenty-five years of sobriety.

Jim knew from his schooling in alcohol and drug studies at UC Santa Cruz that alcohol was not the problem. The problem was that Jim and Laura's interwoven identities were each living out very different lives in different locations, and now the people who knew both Jim and Laura were wondering if the troubling identity issues would ever be resolved.

So the same nagging questions remained unanswered: what had caused the desire for surgery and the ongoing desire to do gender flip-flops? And who was this person: Jim or Laura?

Chapter 8

Multiple Diagnoses

After a year, Jim's contract and corporate-sponsored funding as a counselor with CityTeam in San Jose was up. Looking for other opportunities in his new career, Jim talked with an old friend, Laura's first AA sponsor, Ben. Ben lived in Los Angeles and knew of a job opening at a hospital lock-down psychiatric ward. The patients were dual-diagnosed with major psychiatric issues along with a secondary issue of alcohol or drugs. It paid well, something Jim hadn't seen since his days at Honda. The application dilemma arose again—which name to use? Jim or Laura?

Jim weighed the strengths of each identity in order to choose the right one for the job. Driver's license and legal documents—Laura Jensen. Previous job experience at CityTeam—Jim. Certificate from UC Santa Cruz—Laura. Ah, the deciding factor: the medical center valued the UC Santa Cruz schooling most. Jim applied under the name of Laura, was offered the job, and moved back to Southern California as Laura.

Laura moved into one of the bedrooms in Ben's large house near Beverly Hills. Living and working as Laura was clearly a choice; but even though she wasn't living life as Jim, having a job in a respectable field felt like an important part of the journey to restoration. Now sober three years, Laura felt the Lord at work in this move. Others were not so sure of the wisdom of her choice to work and live as Laura once more.

Jim had had other identities in the past that did not take full control like Laura did, but were all part of a very bizarre co-existence in this one life. The personas of the past were not dominant; they emerged at times when others retreated. The first one, Chrystal West, occurred when Jim was a teenager. As a young adult, Andrea West was active. Starting on the day of the gender surgery, the one named Laura Jensen emerged—she had full control.

Jim felt a sense of failure when he could not stay Jim after leaving his job at Cityteam. During his year at Cityteam, everyone was so excited for his "success" living and working as Jim. Everyone thought Jim was here to stay; but sadly, Jim was gone and Laura was now living in Los Angeles. The name changing had been repeated so many times over the years; most of Jim's good friends were growing weary of it all.

Out of shame at the failure, Laura stopped writing the prayer letters that were such a part of her transparency. However, the prayer team had not given up on what they thought the Lord could do, so they continued to pray for Laura even in the absence of letters.

The job at the medical center psych unit was a good match for Laura. She worked twelve-hour shifts in a hospital environment as a chemical dependency technician. The unit specialized in alcohol and drug recovery for patients with severe psychological disorders, from self-mutilation to schizophrenia and hosts of other issues. Laura's duties included taking vital signs, leading group therapy sessions, and developing daily social events. That included walks around the neighborhood and even lunch at a restaurant for those patients who were capable of contact with the outside world.

The unit had a fabulous psychiatrist, Dr. Allen Rademan who made rounds on the floor once or twice a day. Laura thought he was one of the brightest and most fun medical doctors she had ever met, also one of the best-dressed. This M.D. could have graced the cover of GQ magazine with his fashionable appearance: a class act and a smart guy. As he made his rounds, he frequently asked Laura for her personal impressions of the behaviors of some of the patients on the unit who were struggling with social interaction with other patients.

Laura had been working there about thirty days when Dr. Rademan asked her if he could spend some time interviewing her as the subject. With management approval, over the course of a few weeks, he asked questions about Laura's life, her struggles, and her surgery. He was interested, very interested and asked a bunch of questions no one had ever asked her, ever.

It was puzzling to Laura that Allen Rademan, a prominent well-paid Beverly Hills psychiatric M.D., wanted to give his free time just to talk. What was he looking for? Then Dr. Rademan suggested to Laura she needed to go for further evaluation with other mental health experts to explore the possibility of a "dissociative disorder." Laura stood amazed in silence, and then said, "Okay." Laura did not know what a dissociative disorder was. Dr. Rademan gave her a long list of doctors who could evaluate her in a way that could determine if, in fact, she was suffering from a dissociative disorder.

Laura picked a lady from the list and met with her in her elegantly decorated office on an upper floor of a plush Beverly Hills office building. Carol Waldschmidt, Ph.D., saw Laura for many weeks in order to properly evaluate her. Her evaluation complete, she called Laura to come in to her office to hear the results. "You are indeed suffering from a dissociative disorder, and in fact, you had been exhibiting signs of it from as far back as childhood." Laura still didn't know what this meant. She summoned some courage and asked, "Exactly what is dissociative disorder? I've never heard of it." Dr. Carol said, "Maybe you've heard of multiple personality disorder? It was portrayed in the movies *Sybil* and *Three Faces of Eve*. Dissociative disorder is the current name for what was previously known as multiple personality disorder."

In the psychologist's opinion, the onset of this disorder came as a result of the combination of excessive discipline by her mom and dad, the cross-dressing at the hands of Grandma, and the molestations by Uncle Fred. All the ingredients were there—a textbook recipe for producing dissociative disorder. Escaping to other personalities was a way to survive the pain. The psyche had split into different personalities, each holding a "fragment" of Jim and each having a name: Andrea, Laura, or Chrystal.

Dr. Carol said the surgery was actually performed on a "fragment personality," an "alter" personality, or simply an "alter" who took control of Jim's life from time to time. Unfortunately, the psychologist said, having had the gender changing surgery from male to female would make recovery or restoration of Jim nearly impossible. Psychological treatment was needed to integrate all the personalities into one, thereby eliminating the torment Jim had suffered for almost 40 years.

Laura's head was spinning wildly from the news. Dissociative disorder was all too much to comprehend, especially faced with the conclusion staring her in her face: that changing her gender at the hands of a surgeon, a rather irreversible act, was destruction of the very identity that needed to persevere. Now two different prominent experts were seeing clear indications of Laura having an illness never before considered in all the years of counseling.

Laura was at first completely devastated; and then as she thought about it longer, she thought Dr. Carol could be wrong. Since her specialty was dissociative disorder, perhaps she was biased toward diagnosing it instead of other things. Could it be that her specialty caused her to be prone to looking only for dissociative disorder?

So Laura went to yet another doctor to be evaluated. Laura thought she had a way to set it up so that there would be no upfront bias. She would not disclose to the psychiatrist, Walter K. Heuler, M.D., the diagnosis from the other doctors. But after about three sessions, Dr. Heuler came to the same conclusion, just like the two doctors before him — that Laura had, in fact, been suffering from dissociative disorder.

No longer could Laura deny the diagnosis. The diagnosis was so shocking that she started having frequent panic attacks during the night that left her gasping for breath. Laura could not accept the concept that Laura or Andrea were just fragments, and that the surgery was an error, a mistake. How could Laura continue to live as a fragment person? Laura wanted recovery, but for this she needed help. She needed long-term extensive counseling, and she needed guidance through Jesus Christ.

The psychiatrist who started her down this path, Dr. Alan Rademan from the hospital where she worked, suggested Laura try Prozac, an anti-depressant. But within three days, Laura told him she would not continue taking that drug. With her history of addiction to drugs and alcohol, Laura didn't want to jeopardize her hard-won sobriety by taking any drugs like Prozac. Laura had a healthy aversion to using drugs at all, especially pain pills or drugs to help her cope. Laura thought experiencing the pain was more important than avoiding the pain. Laura knew it was essential for her to maintain her sobriety, and taking prescription mood-changing drugs seemed like a possible road to relapse. Laura would just have to tough it out without drugs, and that was okay with her.

With Dr. Carol Waldschmidt's help, Laura found yet another Ph.D. therapist who specialized in treatment of dissociative disorders. Her name was Margaret Talleth Wright, her office was in Manhattan Beach, California, and the first thing Margaret recommended was that Laura stop indulging the fragment personalities and start trying to live only as Jim. That would make keeping Laura's current job at the hospital impossible. Employers didn't go for people changing genders. So, after only six months working at the hospital psych unit, in compliance with Margaret's request, Laura quit her job and looked for work as Jim.

Jim had an old friend Bill from his early career in the auto industry, who was now in management at Toyota. The office was not far from where Laura was living in Ben's house in Los Angeles. Ever since Jim first developed a friendship with Bill twenty-four years earlier, Bill had always stuck by Jim. As Bill put it, "Jim or Laura, Bozo or whatever you're calling yourself today, you will remain a friend." Jim contacted Bill and asked if Toyota had any jobs that he could do. Bill was straight up with Jim when he said: "With your history, there's no way that Toyota will employ you." But Bill could hire Jim through a temp agency that supplied workers for Toyota. Jim went for it and was hired to work with Bill. Jim was grateful to be back working with his old buddy whom he admired. And, Bill was very happy he could help his old friend Jim at this critical time.

In keeping with his therapist's recommendation to reduce the indulgence of Laura, Jim now presented as Jim at work. That was a big step and commitment toward being Jim. But everywhere else, Jim continued living as Laura. Laura met Ben at her first AA meeting, so Laura felt most comfortable being Laura while living in Ben's home, also at AA meetings. Ben didn't care if Laura left for work in the morning dressed as Jim; he understood. Ben would often laugh and joke about the absurdity of all the switching and personalities.

One of Ben's neighbors, who didn't know about Laura's dual identity, asked Laura for assistance to remove a heavy sliding patio door. Ben went along to observe this heavy work, and later the neighbor pulled Ben aside and said to Ben, "She sure is a strong little thing!" Later Ben's neighbor learned the truth, that Laura was born a man, and the three of them split their sides laughing at his original remark: "She sure is a strong little thing!"

Jim/Laura had five full years of sobriety and was actively working a recovery program which included AA meetings and renting a room in her sponsor's house. He was seeking specialized help to deal with the multiple personality disorder, or the new name, dissociative disorder. He was working as Jim.

Oh, how Jim hated the therapy sessions; they were extremely difficult and very disturbing to the psyche. But he continued to go. He felt that this therapy, unlike the surgery, might finally resolve the over 35-year battle with his gender identity. Margaret Tolleth Wright, Jim's therapist, said that during their sessions, some conducted under hypnosis, she had identified between 13 and 15 separate personalities or personality fragments.

Margaret requested that Jim bring in anything he had signed or written for her to evaluate: notes, journals, any documents with Jim's, Laura's, or Andrea's signature. Margaret was able to show Jim how each different name had a different, distinct writing style. For example, Andrea signed the consent papers for surgery. "Look here," Margaret said, "Andrea's signature is very tight, small, and left-slanted. Now look at Laura's. Laura's is very bold and slanted the opposite way, to the right."

Jim was shocked, until he remembered that almost ten years earlier he had noticed some differences, but did not understand what they meant. Now looking at the physical evidence—the handwriting samples—made it clear.

Jim wondered why it had been so difficult for counselors throughout the years to arrive at, or even consider, the diagnosis of multiple personalities, given the symptoms that were evident all his life. Jim had sought help from the leading specialists, psychologists, and doctors in the field who urged Jim/Laura to have the gender surgery as "treatment" for his disorder.

Jim thought the reason had to do with political correctness. The various people who approved him for surgery, performed the surgery, and later re-affirmed his decision to have surgery were all transgender activists. To an activist, the correct diagnosis for his symptoms of feeling confusion between male and female could only be gender dysphoria. And the only treatment in their opinion for gender dysphoria was gender-change surgery.

For years, Jim had made decisions about his life based completely on having gender dysphoria. Jim was completely devastated by the realization that the radical surgical treatment he underwent and the numerous cosmetic surgeries to make him look female, all done in the name of resolving the issues with the psyche, were actually unnecessary and had the opposite effect—they were very destructive. They had the potential to keep him from ever recovering from the dissociative disorder.

The intensive therapy seemed to make Jim's mind more twisted and confused than ever before. Jim could not trust himself to know who he was sometimes. Jim was tired of it all, tired and completely exhausted. This therapy was very hard work.

In July, 1992, after months of therapy, Jim quit his job at Toyota, stopped the difficult therapy with Margaret Tolleth Wright, and looked for a way to move back to the San Francisco Bay Area, back to Laura's church and the support team, and to be near Roy Thompson and his family. Jim/Laura contacted his former roommate Cathy in the San Francisco area. Cathy had rented Laura a room five years earlier. Cathy knew Laura was struggling again, and Cathy was okay with that. The extra bedroom in her large apartment in Burlingame, close to Jeff's church, was available for rent for the next few months. Cathy invited Laura back as a roommate once again, as Laura again.

Chapter 9

The Return Home

Now that Laura was back to familiar surroundings, she wanted to plug back into Jeff's church where she had the prayer support team. Right away, she contacted Pastor Jeff to let him know all that happened since she left and to alert him that she had changed back to Laura once again. Laura could tell that Jeff was pleased to hear from her, but also detected a little hesitation in his voice this time.

A few days later, Jeff called with some unexpected news. "Laura, I'm sorry. The elders met last night and decided that you are not welcome to return. The elders feel that it is not healthy for the congregation to witness all the changing back and forth between male and female." Jeff tried to soften the blow, "I can't tell you not to come here; it's just a request. The elders would appreciate it if you wouldn't come to church here anymore." Laura was disappointed, but she wasn't angry. Her struggles could be tough to witness and very distracting in a church. Laura knew such visible and bizarre stuff made people uncomfortable. And it wasn't Jeff who wanted Laura gone; he was just relaying the decision of the church elder board, which was protecting the church.

To their credit, the church leadership continued to seek the Lord in reviewing their reaction to Jim's latest disappointing reversal to Laura. Two Mondays later, one of the elders called Laura. "We are having our weekly meeting, and we're calling to tell you we were wrong." Then the most remarkable thing happened. He said, "We want our church to be a place for broken people. Please come back."

I'm on staff in a church myself, and I find what happened next to be the most amazing and wonderful event of all. One by one, the elders took the phone to apologize personally to Laura for telling her she was not welcome.

Laura was crying happy tears, tears of relief and joy. She loved the people in this church. They were closer to her than family. She was scared that they had grown tired of all the difficult twists and turns with Laura and Jim and would find it easy to reject her. For some time she had been living in Los Angeles without a church and she came to realize that she needed the love of her church family. She had pinned her hopes on being welcomed back upon her return to the Bay Area. What a relief that the love of Christ had moved the hearts of the elders to apologize and welcome her back in the church in spite of her ongoing difficulties.

Pastor Jeff and his staff members, Dixie and Pat, thought the response by leadership was great. Roy Thompson had always told Laura, "God is working on both sides of the fence at the same time." That certainly played out in this case. The Lord was working in the lives of the church leadership as well as in Laura's life.

Would this change of heart by the church leadership bring the desired restoration of Jim's life? Or Laura's life?

Laura knew therapy was the only way to get the multiple personalities integrated into one, one persona living for all, and put an end to the switching. Laura selected yet another psychotherapist, this time one near Roy's home who specialized in recovery from dissociative disorders. The therapist determined that working at a normal job for Laura was completely out of the question. The surgery that attempted to eliminate Jim made Laura's case a complicated one. She told Laura, "The surgery almost destroyed Jim, the core of who you are. That makes your recovery very difficult. Don't even think of working for a few years while you focus on your therapy and recovery."

Laura would need some source of income. The federal Supplemental Security Income (SSI) program is designed to help aged, blind, and disabled people who have little or no income. After a one-year waiting period, it provides monthly income to meet basic needs of food, clothing, and shelter. Laura's therapist solicited a written diagnosis letter from each doctor who saw Laura in Los Angeles to strengthen Laura's application for permanent disability under SSI.

The one-year waiting period for the start of SSI disability income was a tough one. Laura's psyche was unsettled by the intensive therapy and her financial situation was dismal. The temporary disability payment from the state was a blessing but not enough to live on.

Yet, God uses our most desperate times to perform the most heart-warming miracles. A man Laura met through Tommy O. was so touched by her story that he secretly changed his last will and testament to leave Laura his old pickup truck and camper. He had cancer and knew his time was short. After he died and Laura received the truck, Tommy gave Laura lots of ribbing about how his longtime friend left Tommy O. nothing, but Laura barely knew him and he bequeathed his truck to her. Laura considered the old pickup and camper a wonderful blessing.

As her therapy continued, Laura alternately lived in the Bay Area at Cathy's or with the Thompsons, and in Murphys with Tommy O. or with the young coffee shop owners. At times, the camper provided a roof over her head.

The relationships continued to grow for Laura in the little California Gold Country town. The coffee shop had grown to be a full restaurant, and the young couple who owned it allowed Laura to run errands in exchange for meals. Laura needed some help and she preferred to do something to help others in exchange for food, which was cool. In an act of incredible generosity, the owners set aside a room in their home for Laura. She had been spending the cold winter nights in the hills of Murphys in her unheated camper. This family made sure Laura became part of their family and always included Laura with the family. They even entrusted Laura to baby-sit their young daughter.

Being on the receiving end of such generosity was a humbling experience, but such generosity made life in this season very nice and Laura accepted it with thanks.

Time with these families made Laura feel almost normal. Being surrounded by all the good people in normal living situations helped Laura see the model of normal people and how her masquerade as a woman was not real at all. Healthy relationships, seen up close, have enormous positive impact through modeling.

Somewhere during the following months, her daughter tentatively allowed her dad Jim (not Laura) back into her life, too. It was a fresh start.

Roy remembers Laura from this time:

Laura had always brought an incredible gift of laughter to our home. She had a tremendous capacity to joke about her experience. It was a welcome relief valve. Many times our laughter was so deep it brought us to tears.

And perseverance. Laura continued to journal, and to seek help, spiritually and emotionally. Her desire for wholeness never ceased.

Multiple personality disorder, or dissociative disorder as it is now called, was the key. The other diagnoses did not fit because they were wrong. Hope at last. All the pieces were falling in place. Finally, the bright light at the end of a very long tunnel. Jim spent another year in therapy

integrating the personalities and peace came as a welcome guest to his soul.
—*Roy Thompson*

Laura was puzzled by not remembering much detail of the tough therapy sessions trying to unravel the dissociative disorder. I'm told that's part of this disorder—missing pieces in one's memories. Laura would remember more from the sessions with the Christian psychologists because it was less invasive and focused on things such as childhood issues and working a program of sobriety.

Working with the Christian counselor on recovery issues, Laura prepared her personal inventory, the fourth step of any 12-step program. Most people write a few pages, maybe ten, to identify resentments, pain, and unresolved issues of their past that they are ready to turn over to their higher power. Laura's account for this fourth step was over a hundred pages long. The therapy session lasted four hours, ending with the counselor and Laura in the parking lot, where they set fire to one hundred plus pages. The pages burned and floated away in the light breeze. Symbolically letting all the pain and resentments go, forever.

As the ashes were smoldering and a gentle breeze lifted them upward, Laura felt a strong sense of relief and lightness, as if she had been liberated from all the heavy weight of the previous years. The psychologist and Laura returned back to his office for prayer. As the psychologist started to pray for Laura, Laura had a very personal encounter with Jesus, a powerful spiritual experience. In Laura's vision she came face-to-face with Jesus. He was dressed all in white, with His feet hidden under His robe. As the Lord approached her, His arm stretched out, His face with a smile, Laura saw herself as a baby. At that very moment, He scooped up Laura in His arms and said, "You are now safe with Me forever." She was in His arms and together they were moving upward out of the vision. Then the vision was over. Tears streamed down Laura's cheeks, a smile on her face.

Laura did not remember what words her therapist prayed on that special day, but she sure remembers her face-to-face encounter with the Lord and His words, "You are now safe with Me forever." She knew at that moment recovery and restoration were now in the Lord's hands. Finally, Laura was sure that recovery and restoration would come. The Lord had come to her, scooped her up and now and forever was holding her in His arms. She would be restored.

But this would take time and Laura needed to qualify for federal disability. A government-assigned group of disability doctors extensively evaluated Laura over a week-long period. The process required Laura to perform a series of written and oral exams with a different doctor for each test. This group of doctors also concluded that Laura had been suffering from dissociative disorder all her life. This diagnosis raises skepticism among some, but nonetheless the panel of doctors assigned to evaluate Laura by the federal government approved her for permanent disability as a result of all the testing. Laura qualified to live in a federal housing complex and receive a check each month. Now Laura was free to pursue treatment for her disorder with an open-ended time frame.

Laura continued her therapy and AA meetings, and her faith that Christ could restore her broken, twisted life grew immensely. A turning point in her counseling occurred when Laura acknowledged that she was not a real person, but just a fragment.

The Bible says the truth will set you free. Jim received a double dose that day. First was the acknowledgement of the truth—Laura was only one fragment of Jim. The second truth arrived in a letter from Dr. Walker, the expert who had approved Jim for surgery, in response to a letter Jim had written to him about having dissociative disorder and being an alcoholic at the time of the approval. In the letter, Dr.

Walker revealed, "I assure you that I share, as best I can, some of your pain that *this mistake* has caused to you" (italics mine).

Jim clung to the revelation. Seeing the word "mistake" in a letter from the expert in the field of gender change surgery, the very one who approved Jim for surgery, gave Jim an important piece of truth. The surgery was all a mistake, performed as treatment for a disorder Jim didn't have: gender dysphoria. Jim wasn't a man trapped in a woman's body. Jim was an alcoholic with dissociative disorder trying to escape the pain of his childhood.

Jim's experience illustrates the point that the diagnosis and evaluation process for sex changing surgery was very seriously flawed. Even today, rarely do therapists go deep to discover what issues are causing patients to express the intense desire to disfigure their bodies and change their identities. The therapist's answer is surgery, without taking the time and hard work required to determine what unresolved and undiagnosed disorder might be underneath the strongly-held compulsion to do away with one's identity.

Jim's experience also illustrates the importance of putting faith and hope in Jesus and the importance of having a church that will not turn its back on the "scary" person. Pastor Jeff's church did not lose hope that Jesus would ultimately work everything out in Laura for her good. Laura, though weary, never gave up on Jesus and as a result was encouraged by an encounter with Jesus in prayer.

But Jim stayed away from the church family that for years had supported Laura in prayer, with love, and financially, as well. It was the old story—that was Laura's church; Jim, male persona, had never attended it. Now he felt it would be too awkward, and Laura would fight him.

But in a moment of confidence, Jim checked with Pastor Jeff to see if it would be okay for Jim to come to church. The answer to that question from Jeff and the elders resulted in one of the most memorable, supportive days of Jim's life, where he felt the full support of the entire church, cheering him on to resolve his gender conflict. Pastor Jeff crafted his entire Sunday message around Jim's story as his way to introduce Jim to the church family who had known him only as Laura.

As Pastor Jeff tells it in his own words:

One day Jim called and said he wanted to come back to church. He said God had healed him. Laura was gone and he missed his church. Through all the years of instability, he had only attended as Laura. Obviously, this needed careful thought and prayer for its impact on both Jim and the Body.

It was thrilling to hear the change and confidence in Jim's voice, but I was fearful that he might be setting himself up for failure if Laura reemerged. I wanted to celebrate with Jim what God had done but wondered if he would be better served by preserving this extended period of stability. My strongest feeling wanted to protect him.

I told him the elders and I needed to think and pray about it. After discussing it at length, we felt it was most important to honor what God had done in Jim and let the Body share in that. Playing it safe out of fear of reaction or failure seemed a lack of faith.

We selected a Sunday and put much preparation and prayer into it. I preached on God's great love for great sinners. Focusing on the story of Zaccheus, I catalogued how throughout Scripture God has drawn people whose lives were such a mess that no one could have imagined they could be changed. In fact, so often these were God's "chosen."

Then I told Jim's story of abuse, addiction and poor choices, including the tragic step of gender change surgery. The focus was God's great work–changing someone we could never imagine. I wanted them to share in the thrill of a great work God had done and was doing in our midst. Then I introduced Jim.

The response was overwhelming. Every person in the room immediately stood and applauded. It was the most dramatic acknowledgement of God's power I have ever experienced. Then Jim spoke powerfully of God's grace in his life. Standing next to him, I was sobbing openly as were all the elders and the many others who had prayed and stood with Jim through his courageous and painful journey.

I know it went beyond what anyone thought they would encounter in church that day. It went beyond what most imagined could even happen. The reason for the impact that day was that everyone knew that God had done a miraculous work.

Jim says that day had a huge impact on him. Being free to openly celebrate all that God had done launched him forward in his growth and recovery. That day also had a tremendous impact on the church. It affirmed that God was at work among us. It clarified again that the church's priority was being a place of healing amidst the mess of life. It focused us on worshipping the Lord for the great trophy of grace Jim was.

We made it clear that God's work in Jim was far from done. We acknowledged that Jim's experience was far beyond what most of us could understand. But we celebrated as a Body that God had done a miraculous work in our midst. What a great day it was.

—Pastor Jeff Farrar

Jim continued his intensive therapy, and drew ever closer to Jesus Christ, and stayed sober. That didn't mean it was easy. The years from 1992 through 1996 were very difficult. Jim was back on the yo-yo of bouncing between living as Jim and then Laura, changing jobs each time he changed persona.

Jim found work as a salesman at a small oil company thanks to a friend Patrick, who also worked there. Jim was successful but Patrick had a proposal. He wanted to start a trucking company hauling gasoline, and he wanted Jim to go in with him. They incorporated the company, got a checking account, and started looking for rental property for a small office and space to keep two or three gasoline trucks. A longtime friend of Patrick's advanced him $190,000.

They were only weeks away from opening when a friend from church called Jim to say that Patrick had placed a plastic bag over his head and suffocated himself because of a failed relationship with a longtime girlfriend. Again, as a coping response, Jim retreated back to being Laura and found a job in a coffee shop.

During this five year period, several of Jim's closest personal friends and supporters died. His great friend Jon Thompson, Roy's son, who waited for Laura at the bus stop in his wheelchair when she was living with the Thompson family, was diagnosed with AIDS. This dreadful illness was transmitted to him through a blood transfusion done years before—before the medical community was aware of the need to test the blood supply. He had been paralyzed in a freak accident at age nine—hit by a car while standing on the sidewalk. That was tragedy enough; but now suddenly at 29 years of age, he was gone, a casualty of someone else's illness transmitted through the public blood supply.

Jim's longtime counselor, Dr. Dennis Guernsey, was diagnosed with brain cancer and died shortly after his last visit with him. Then Cathy, who gave Laura her first place to stay after leaving the recovery house, was diagnosed with colon cancer at age 46. The growth wasn't discovered until well after it had spread throughout her internal organs. She lost weight fast and was hospitalized frequently. During that time, large numbers of Cathy's friends surrounded her to offer support, including her friend Karen.

Most of Cathy's friends knew the Jim/Laura story. If Jim or Laura hung around with anyone long enough, it became awkward to keep the secret. With Jim's permission, Cathy told Karen about his surgery and that Laura was born a man but had been switching back and forth between Laura and Jim. It did not seem very shocking or important to her. That was good with Jim, to have another person who knew and accepted his story, someone who was safe.

Cathy, Karen, and Jim went out for a meal together every once in awhile. With Cathy being so sick, Karen and Jim started getting together more and more to have coffee and to cope with Cathy's terminal illness. They did not know it but the Lord was at work, slowly knitting their hearts together during this time of great difficulty. The Lord was revealing His plan for the recovery and restoration of Jim, and Karen was a key. Neither Jim nor Karen could see this coming, at least not yet. And Jim couldn't quite grasp the wild idea that God was that BIG or would restore that part of his broken life. But Jim seemed to have a little hop to his step whenever Karen was around.

Relationships were extremely important to Jim. They helped him feel like a normal person and that helped in stabilizing the identity of Jim. Pastor Jeff and the ladies on staff at the church, Pat and Dixie, were constant and continuous support, as well as Roy Thompson and his family. They all believed that the Lord was powerful enough to heal Laura and restore Jim to his true identity in Christ as Jim.

Even though Laura was on permanent SSI disability and living in federal housing, Jim knew the Lord wanted him to trust this part of his life to Jesus, and not to depend on government handouts. So Jim contacted his good friend Ed, this time for a job as Jim. Ed didn't have any openings at the body shop this time, but he was on the board of directors of a machine shop. Ed got it done; Jim was offered a job as a delivery driver, with the promise of advancement. This was very cool and a great fit for Jim in returning to his male persona.

Jim wanted to carve out his own path in life, not exist on a handout, so he took the job. He moved out of the very nice federal housing in Murphys, knowing he never ever wanted to return to such a dependent lifestyle. Jim moved back into the Thompsons' home in Pleasanton, an easy commute to his new job at the machine shop.

Now the fog was starting to lift. It was clear that all the prayers and perseverance were starting to bring the fruit of the spirit and were transforming this once broken life.

Chapter 10

Joined in Love

As Cathy's health continued to fail her, she was hospitalized more frequently. The Lord was using Cathy's illness to draw her friends Karen and Jim into a relationship in a way only the Lord can do. Jim hated being in hospitals; so when Cathy was in the hospital, he invited Karen to go with him to visit her.

This "Jim" identity was gaining strength and having a friendship with Karen was helping. Jim was enjoying who he was becoming, and he was especially aware of this when he was with Karen. Jim knew this was the right time to have the one key piece of legal identification restored, his birth record. After the gender changing surgery, Jim had petitioned the courts to change his birth certificate to Laura, female. Now that he was completely sure of the truth—his original birth name and birth gender were correct—Jim wanted to change his birth certificate back to Jim, male. One more step to take in the journey home.

Jim found an attorney and together they developed a strategy. Certainly, if they gave the court affidavits prepared by a surgeon and a psychologist stating that Jim was a male, the court would rule in his favor. The affidavits would have to be written very strongly, leaving no question about his gender being male. Jim and his attorney felt that the strongest case could be made by the same people who approved and performed Jim's gender changing surgery years before. The doctors complied and each prepared an affidavit to the Superior Court which stated that Jim was and is a male, even though he underwent surgery that changed his appearance.

Unfortunately, it didn't work. The law in California for changing the gender on a birth certificate specified a one-way trip. The only way to change it back was to undergo "reversal" surgery. The cost and risk of the surgery was out of the question for Jim. For now, the door to restoring the birth certificate to his original birth gender was closed.

But I find the surgeon's acknowledgement in his statement to the court to be startling. Follow this closely. By declaring that Jim was still a male and that the surgery did not change him into a woman, the surgeon was stating that the type of surgery he was performing on men on a daily basis does not work—it does not change a man into a woman.

Surgeons are not at all held accountable to provide proof that they change the birth gender through surgery. A DNA test done post-operatively would prove no gender/sex change takes place during this surgical procedure. The courts routinely use DNA to prove innocence or guilt in cases of murder and rape, why not for gender? Perhaps the time has come to use DNA as the standard in our courts to determine gender identity in order to change documents such as birth certificates and driver's licenses.

Jim desperately wanted his legal identity to be male, even without a restored birth certificate. He was falling in love with Karen and realized his inaccurate birth certificate could be an insurmountable hurdle to a future with her. There must be something else he could do. Jim racked his brain trying to devise other strategies that might work. Jim had the affidavits from the doctors. It failed in court, but could it be used to get some other type of identification instead of the birth certificate? He could register to vote as Jim—that didn't have a gender specified on it. The Social Security Administration was willing to change his name back to Jim and issue a replacement card. Together the voter registration card and the Social Security card could be used to get a new driver's license. Step by step, Jim built up a portfolio of documents in the name of Jim, with the male identity.

With the voter registration, doctors' affidavits, driver's license, Social Security card, passport photo and application clutched tightly in his hand, Jim waiting in the long line at the downtown passport office—San Francisco, where anything goes. Finally, it was Jim's turn to walk up to the window. This was the big test. Were the documents Jim had in his hand enough?

Jim gave the documents to the man at the window. When the guy researched Jim's Social Security record, it showed him as female. This was just awful. The man at the window said that he could not issue Jim a passport with a male identity, but he could prepare a passport as Jim, female. How crazy is this? Well, his entire life was crazy—why should this day be any different? Destroying the true real identity after surgery had been so easy. Restoring it back was proving to be impossible.

Jim calmly collected his thoughts and asked the guy if he could see a supervisor. A tall, slender, older woman walked to the window. "I'm the supervisor. How can I help you?" she said. With a quivering voice and trembling hands, Jim spoke very slowly, even haltingly. It was hard to breathe or catch his breath. He felt as if everything was on the line. Jim slowly unfolded the documents and told her the long difficult story and how important it was to have a passport showing Jim, male. Jim was almost in tears when she gently laid her hand on top of his as it rested on the window's edge. She said, "Sweetie, I'm going to take care of this for you. You will have your passport as Jim, male, as requested. Don't you worry, this needs to be done." This nice lady prepared a new passport for Jim as male.

And so it was. The angel at the passport office did what the judge would not do—restored Jim's legal identity to Jim, male. Jim may never be able to get his birth certificate to read correctly, but the passport works just as well.

The Lord was clearly answering years of prayer and fulfilling His promise to restore Jim's badly broken life. Only the Lord could have provided that supervisor at the passport office to honor Jim's request for the passport change. Only the Lord could have painstakingly brought Jim through the painful, tangled, and convoluted process to heal his psyche and end his confusion. Only the Lord could have inspired his friend Ed to take another chance on him and recommend Jim for a job that held the promise of a new career.

December of 1996 held the promise of exciting new opportunities with a promising new job for Jim and an unexpected invitation from Karen to attend her employer's Christmas party. Was Jim on a date? Picking Karen up in his car, Jim felt a little awkward at first, being out with Karen; but she assured Jim, "We are just buddies." She assured Jim this was not a date.

Jim and Karen were getting to be close friends, able to confide in each other about personal struggles partly because they prayed together so frequently for their sick friend, Cathy.

Jim was starting to believe in miracles—he could not deny that the tide of trouble was beginning to turn. What a string of amazing developments: his passport now issued in the name of Jim, male; his exciting new opportunity at the machine shop; and the joy of developing a relationship with Karen. Jim was like a kid; his little feet could not stay on the ground. Truly the power and grace of Jesus Christ were at work.

Karen was a computer "geek." Jim was anything but technical; he had a hard time even with a TV remote. While working at the machine shop, Jim saved his money and purchased a used Apple laptop computer. Jim soon discovered a wireless Internet service called "Ricochet." Ricochet was an ISP, an internet service provider, but with a capability that was ahead of its time: wireless in the Bay Area at a time when wireless networking simply didn't exist. By using the Ricochet box attached with Velcro strips to the laptop lid, Jim could send and receive email anywhere in the San Francisco Bay area. Jim was able to drop an email to Karen when he was just sitting in a coffee shop—something he did frequently—or during his lunch hour while sitting in his car. Jim was having fun, sending little love notes via e-mail to Karen. The romance was now in full bloom and Jim, the "non-geek," found being part of the email community to be a bunch of fun. One such email Jim sent to Karen at 5:06 a.m. read:

> You know, I'm gonna have to admit it, although I should wait until I see you in person...I love you more than I ever thought it possible to love another person.

Several times a day, Jim and Karen sent emails like that back and forth. In one of Karen's email responses to Jim, when he says "what a wonderful place to be, just near you," she writes, "I still can't absorb that you'll always be there for me. I'm there for you too.–Karen"

Jim discovered that Karen's birthday was in mid-January, so in a gutsy move he called Karen and asked if she would like to have dinner on her birthday. To Jim's joyful surprise, she said yes. They enjoyed a wonderful dinner, laughed, and talked. After paying the bill, Jim stood up as if to walk out, but Karen stayed seated. She looked up at Jim with a mischievous smile and said, "Do you know what you just did?" Alarmed and befuddled, thinking he must have committed some grievous dating error, Jim plopped back down and asked, "No, what did I do?" She replied, "You just did a date!" Then they both howled with laughter.

Jim was now living in amazement over the new life he was carving out with Karen, and it was downright fun, too. He tried to see her every few days—Jim was falling hard for Karen. Jim took her to a movie and, feeling like a teenager, placed his hand gently over her hand and hung on for dear life. It was electric. By early February, they were both aware that the Lord was weaving their hearts together.

Jim had not been in any relationship of any kind, not even a date, for fifteen years—since his first marriage ended. Jim's life had revolved around staying sober so he could get well. The extent of Jim's social life was attending AA meetings and church. He had no desire for romantic involvement until Karen came along. Jim was far too depressed in all the years since his surgery to desire any romantic relationships. Switching back and forth between Jim and Laura made it impossible to even consider having other relationships. Thankfully, homosexuality was not an issue, never had been.

Now a miracle was unfolding that was beyond Jim's wildest imagination. Being in a romantic relationship with Karen was making Jim feel different about himself. Only the Lord could have begun this weaving together of two very different lives, begun with praying together for Cathy. There was an undeniable explosion of love between them. They could not explain it. They couldn't understand it; but they both sure could feel it, and knew there was nothing like it. Jim knew it was love, the love the Lord places on your heart for one special lady at one very special season in life; this was it with Karen and Jim.

Jim and Karen drove to the Los Angeles area to introduce her to his daughter and his mother. As they were saying the final good-byes, Jim's daughter whispered in Karen's ear, "Thanks for taking care of my dad." This struck Jim as an amazing acknowledgment of his daughter's desire to see her dad restored.

On February 18, at a candlelight dinner at Karen's home, she finally admitted to Jim he was her "boyfriend." For the past month, she had been understandably cautious, reluctant to commit too quickly and maybe change her mind and cause him hurt. But now she was sure. Boyfriend. Knock Jim over with a feather; he was blown away. His feet were totally unable to touch the ground.

By now Jim and Karen had known each other for almost five years. Jim knew her strength was in the Lord, as was his. They were determined to do this courtship the Lord's way.

Roy and Bonita didn't try to hide their absolute delight and approval, with such remarks as: "Our backyard makes a terrific setting for a wedding." Jim met Karen's friends and went to several counseling sessions with her Christian counselor. Karen wanted everyone to get to know her new beau, and to affirm her choice.

On Easter Sunday, Jim prepared a long letter he would read to Karen that expressed his desire to take her for his wife; he knew she would say "Yes" and she did. They set the wedding date: May 18, only six weeks later.

The happy couple had to work fast to get through the pre-marital counseling program that Karen's pastor required. The counseling included taking tests to evaluate compatibility and maturity for marriage. They scored off the charts to the pastor's surprise and to each other's delight. These two lovebirds were giggly, dreamily, and rip-roaringly joyous together as they planned the big wedding day celebration.

The wedding would be at the Thompsons' home, where 12 years earlier a depressed Laura tentatively stood on the front steps, broken beyond description. Now the garden at their house would be the setting for a celebration of a restored life and two lives joined in marriage, with Roy officiating.

Without a doubt, the power and grace of Jesus had pulled this one off.

Jeff Farrar remembers the day —

It was a blazing hot day as Jim and I stood together before Roy Thompson in his backyard. He was the groom and I was the best man. Next to Jim was a beautiful, glowing Karen. A group of family and friends had gathered to witness their wedding.

As I stood there looking at Jim, I remembered another scene. It was Easter dinner, shortly after Laura had come into our lives. I was looking out from my kitchen to the living room. There on the couch were my 90-year-old grandmother, my mom, and Laura, all dressed up for Easter, sitting on the couch chatting, as our three kids played with my dad on the floor.

Susan, my wife, and I were in the kitchen preparing food. We looked at each other, and began to giggle. Our extended family knew nothing about Laura other than that she was a friend. We were convinced that sharing our family with Laura was absolutely the correct thing to do. Yet we were struck by how following the Lord had put us in such an unusual circumstance. We were in no way ashamed of Laura. In fact, we were proud of the steps she had taken and the growth we could see. Yet we had no idea how Laura's life would unfold. All we knew was the Lord was at work.

Standing in the Thompsons' backyard years later, seeing Jim and Karen hold hands and commit their lives to each other before the Lord, I was struck by God's goodness and faithfulness to all of us. I felt overwhelmed at the privilege of having witnessed God's miraculous power in creating a trophy of grace.

— Pastor Jeff Farrar

As an author I could not have come up with a more powerful conclusion to this long twisted journey of Jim's than Jeff as best man at his wedding—it was perfect. Jeff Farrar, the pastor who never gave up on that "scary," unlovable, broken life. Jeff, who went out of his way and encouraged a whole congregation to support Laura or Jim. Jeff says his job was to love the broken people, and it was God's job to transform their lives.

Maid of honor was Cathy, dear friend to both Karen and Jim. Visibly the cancer was taking Cathy's health, and less than two months later she was gone. In attendance were all the members of the formerly secret prayer team, church elders, family members and loving friends who walked with Jim from brokenness to wholeness. Truly this was the Lord's day to celebrate a victory; His blessings were written in every smile on every face.

Only God could have placed a woman like Karen in Jim's life, allowing them to become friends first, and then weaving them together along the way to marriage. What a joyous day it was, May 18, 1997, in the Thompsons' garden in Pleasanton, two lives joined together in marriage in the presence of all who never gave up—pastors, friends, and faithful supporters, all cheering approval.

To the glory of God, the struggle with psychological disorder was over and a new life was beginning. Jim was now the man he wanted to be and the man God created him to be. That is as good as it gets.

Even though Jim and Karen faced unusual issues in beginning a life together, they had a great head start by knowing that marriage is a commitment of a man and a woman to each another, and both to Jesus Christ. And it did happen—to Jim's absolute amazement! In our backyard, in front of a hundred guests, they had the wedding of a lifetime. God in His "more than you could ever ask or think" way, provided Jim with an amazing companion named Karen. To watch their love for each other grow is a marvelous reminder that God's grace is alive; it is sufficient; it is beyond our understanding!

    —Dr. Roy Thompson

Chapter 11

The Lord Prevailed

It had been twelve tough years since Laura first arrived at the front steps of the Thompsons', despondent and wanting to end her life. Now restored and standing in the Thompson backyard was Jim, a man getting married and preparing to start a fresh new life with his wonderful bride, Karen.

That day, without a doubt, was the most wonderful day of my life. Yes, I did say "my" life because I am not just the author but I am also "Laura" and "Jim" in this story. All the years of prayer and dedication to loving this once "scary," broken person paid off big and gave birth to a servant of God, now on staff at a large church.

I'm one of those scary people, restored to life and perfected with love through the extravagant grace of Christ. Only the love of people connected to the power and grace of Christ can produce such amazing results. So, when you come face to face with a "scary" or unusual person, remember this story. Do not consider "scary" people as unredeemable; think instead that God knows no such boundaries.

As I relived all the twists and turns sharing this story as a third party, I could see how the power of God's love shown through "His people" truly transformed my life. It was not a movie, it was, in fact, my life—every twisted, painful detail as my account of the long journey. Finally, Christ came in a prayer, scooped me up, and held me in His arms. The resulting restoration to health is the proof of His power to transform lives.

Now that you know it was me, I will use my name, Walt. After all, I've become accustomed to name changes. This once "scary" person who was told, "We don't want your kind in our church" now serves God as the Director of Care Ministries in a large Southern California church. It is perhaps hard to imagine the Lord could have big plans for such a "scary," unusual person as I once was, but He sure did.

After a long, tortuous struggle, I returned to my male birth gender and got married to my best friend Kaycee (her nickname since college—a spelled-out version of her initials K.C., first name Karen). I have been married now 12 years, sober over 22 years. I'm a spring chicken at 68.

For me, being invited to join the church staff as the Director of Care Ministries was not a slam dunk at all. My interview process unhinged a few people and challenged church pastors and elders. After all, for the elders and pastors to say "Yes, come join our staff" to this former transgender took significant discussions, prayer, and conviction by the Lord. Their decision process was difficult, and it took a full year to process the possibility of adding someone with my history to the staff. The move felt very risky to the church because the reputation of the church in the community was at stake. But it was not my prowess at interviews that made the difference; rather it was my first book "Trading My Sorrows." As each elder read my account of my struggles and the Lord's redeeming power in my life, it became clear to them that I had been uniquely prepared to fill the Director of Care position at church.

They read Pastor Jeff's account of his process in dealing with the challenge of welcoming Laura as a transgender in the church, and it provided them with another way to approach the decision. In Pastor Jeff's words:

Upon hearing Laura's story, many have asked what principles we at the church used that could help other pastors and church leaders when encountering people in extraordinary situations. I refer to them as "scary" people not because they are "scary," but because their situations and experience are so outside of ours that they scare us. We simply do not know what to do with them. For many Christian leaders, anything outside of our experience makes us nervous; we measure ourselves on knowing what to do. To this day, Walt encounters Christians, especially leaders, who when they hear his story, are frightened. This often results in their rejection, and even attack, out of lack of understanding and a need to protect their church and their world.

One danger in looking back over years of a journey in ministry is to put an overly positive spin on things. From this end of the story, it looks wonderful and our instincts and wisdom get magnified. The truth is that the great majority of the time, we were operating with no experience and little understanding of how things would turn out. We were scrambling to stay faithful to our call to lead and protect the church while struggling to engage Laura/Walt in love and truth. The dominant feeling was how uncertain the future was and how out of control everything looked to us. That isn't a comfortable feeling, but we were convinced that ministry of the Spirit often looks and feels just like that.

God used a "scary" person to accomplish His work in us individually and corporately.

—Pastor Jeff Farrar

Since Pastor Jeff and his church found having such a person among the congregation to be challenging, how could anyone blame a large church for backing away from filling an important staff leadership position with a former transsexual? The decision required even greater scrutiny by church leadership than simply allowing a transgender person to attend church. The decision to employ a person with such a history would require much prayer and poring over Scriptures to seek the Lord's guidance.

The real issue for most churches is they have no experience or history with a transgender in their midst who has been restored by Christ. The willingness of any church to welcome such "scary" people to join the staff will depend on the senior pastor and perhaps all the combined personal life experience of the leadership. For the most part, such a dilemma is not an experience they would ordinarily embrace with open arms.

As for me, when I read the qualifications and the job description for the position of care director, I was thinking that Christ had uniquely prepared me for exactly this time and He could use my twisted journey and subsequent recovery and my certificate in alcohol and drug recovery to serve him in this very special way. I applied in August of 2005. The scrutiny and interview process started but stalled about two months later. My history, however uniquely designed, posed significant concerns for a church that was in recovery itself from the most difficult period of its history–a public scandal by the former senior pastor. Now a person who at one time had been a transsexual was applying for a staff position. This was not an easy prospect for the elders or pastors who wanted to protect the church and stay out of the media limelight.

I asked my pastor, Pastor Rick, to provide his thoughts and reflections into the process that eventually made it possible for the church to employ a former transsexual.

As a pastor in a large church in Southern California, I see many people that are scary. Walt was one of those people. Not because of how he looked but because of his past. We had a position open for Care Director in our church, and Walt applied for the position. Not knowing about Walt's past, I interviewed him for the job. Based on his abilities and skills he seemed like he would be a great candidate.

I was feeling really good about Walt; and then the following day, a person in our church told me about his past and that I should ask him about it. I immediately called Walt and asked him to enlighten me. Well, that's exactly what he did for the next hour as he shared with me his journey of confusion, addiction, and then finding himself. Throughout the journey, God was pursuing him and calling him to a life of love and completeness.

As I heard Walt's story, I was moved both because of the pain he had gone through and my own compassion for another human being. I knew that not everyone in the church would feel as I did, and that it would be a process to bring him on in this position.

I was right! It took a year of multiple meetings with church leadership as well as individual meetings to talk through having a person like this on staff. All those involved were good people that wanted the best for the church and Walt. All believed that God could transform anyone from any past. The difficulty was, should we put a person like this in a leadership position?

My argument was: how is Walt's past any more disqualifying then that of the Apostle Paul? Remember Paul? Before following Jesus he persecuted any who claimed to follow Jesus. Paul was probably the scariest person of his day; and yet, after surrendering his life to Jesus, he had the biggest leadership impact. If that is true, then why couldn't that be the case with Walt?

We finally came to agree that we all meet Jesus at the cross and He washes away our sins so that we can be used by God for His purposes. Since God doesn't look back but instead sees our potential for the future, we needed to do the same thing with Walt. So later that week, I went with my wife, Bobbi, to meet with Walt at his place of employment, a coffee shop. I asked him if he was ready to have a larger impact in the lives of people than serving them coffee. He said, "What do you mean?" I said, "Our leadership team all agreed to offer you the job." He was so excited and asked, "When do I start?"

Over the last two years, God has used Walt's past experiences to create a Care Ministry that really helps people move to wholeness. The good news is that if God can do this for Walt, He can do it for you and the people you encounter as well.

—Pastor Rick Bailard

Someone like me will always need pastors like Rick and Jeff who can see beyond my twisted past. The result in my case is a remarkable testimony. I am so grateful that neither of them gave up on me.

Don Bennett was and is the chairman of the elder board that considered the decision to hire me. Don tells of the process:

The church elder board was asked to consider hiring a gentleman named Walt Heyer as our Care Pastor, a position which required leading a department comprised of several key ministries such as Celebrate Recovery, the benevolence ministry, and visiting the ill and dying. We had no idea what God had in store for us.

We were fully apprised of Walt's qualifications as far as leadership. We were then given all the information regarding his personal journey; and to be honest, we were taken back. We were very hesitant to even consider hiring him, but our pastors Bob Thune and Rick Bailard were strongly in favor of his hiring, and deemed him to be well qualified. They repeatedly emphasized the grace and forgiveness of God, regardless of the depth of depravity in anyone's life. We read about the biblical hero David, but tend not to dwell on the fact that he was a murderer and an adulterer...look how God used him and how much we lift him up as a hero! The truth is the Bible says that David was a man after God's own heart! The lesson for us is that we need to see people as God sees them, not how we perceive them! When an individual has been touched by the Holy Spirit, he is never the same person! The book of Romans is clear about that. It states that when a man is "in Christ" that he is a new creature; the person he used to be is no longer, and he is a brand new creation. When God changes a man, it is permanent.

There were pastors on staff and elders who were adamant that he would be a liability and that hiring him would cause the church damaging publicity. How would the church leadership handle the backlash when people found out about his troubled past and questioned our decision to hire him?

We tabled the discussion and prayed. It was too big a decision to make without further thought and prayer. For the time being, the answer was "No."

Months later, the matter came before the board again. The same responses were repeated. Questions like, "Can we hire someone with his background? It seems like such a liability. What if he falls back into the same lifestyle? What will our congregation think? What if his background becomes public? How transparent do we have to be? Are we being prudent? Are we being hypocrites?"

Once again, we tabled the discussion and went to prayer. I felt like God was testing us, and I was uncomfortable because I wanted to do what God would do, but felt that protecting the church was my duty also. Was I getting in His way? Maybe. Just maybe.

All the time we were agonizing over this decision, Walt was writing his life story for publication. When the book came out, he quietly gave me a copy to read. I read the book in a matter of hours the same night. It was a difficult read for me as I read one tragic chapter after another. But then... the good news and the happy ending! As I read Pastor Jeff Farrar's "Thoughts on Ministering to Scary People," I was overwhelmed with grief. I, of all people, who had been saved at age 42 after leading a life of sin and devoid of God, had been holding back grace and forgiveness to Walt Heyer? Give me a break! Were we as leaders forgetting that we also were saved by God's grace? And, who are we to determine which sins are worse than others? Isn't a life saved by grace enough to cover the sins of the past?

I began to feel a burden being taken off my shoulders and my spiritual eyes opening by the power of the Holy Spirit...it was a freeing experience. I had no fear of my decision and knew that we needed to hire this godly man.

I called Walt and asked him to sell me 15 copies of his book. As I gave one to each of the elders and pastors, I asked them, "Please read this book before our next meeting. I am placing the topic of hiring Walt on the agenda one more time." My heart was beating rapidly, and I was confident that God was at work.

When the board and pastors met again, I could sense a change. Elders were forced to think about their own sinfulness and God's forgiveness towards them. They had to evaluate their own inner prejudices, take a look at their own lack of forgiveness toward others and their failure to reach out to another sinner and embrace him.

This process was definitely God-ordained. In order for faith to grow, it must be tested. In this instance, the Lord challenged the faith of an entire leadership team. Walt told me later that the Lord took him and Kaycee to a new level in their faith as well.

We have never looked back and questioned the ultimate decision to hire Walt. He has been a blessing to our church and to the people around him. I am privileged to not only

know him and Kaycee, but I am grateful to God that He imparted His wisdom on a leadership team who was in such need of wisdom. God never ceases to amaze me how He uses imperfect and needy people to accomplish His will. What a marvelous thing it is to be used by Him for His purposes!
  —*Don Bennett, Chairman of the Elder Board*

Chapter 12

Kaycee Shares Her Story

When our mutual friend Cathy shared with me the nature of Walt's struggle, I was shocked—I had never heard of anyone having this kind of surgery, or this kind of problem. Even though I really didn't know Walt, my heart went out to him.

I tended to gravitate toward people who weren't perfect, people who had struggled through complex issues and come out the other side, people with life wisdom gained the hard way. My own maturing process had been a struggle, with years of therapy required to learn how to "be." My marriage of 13 years ended in divorce, which, while done in a "civilized" manner, was painful. I had no children, just me and like single women everywhere, my cat. And I had a big plus: a new relationship with God, specifically Jesus Christ.

Having been single for several years already, I was determined to focus first on my relationship with Jesus Christ, and second on learning how to form healthy relationships. With the assistance of a counselor, I doggedly pursued any hurts or hang-ups that held me back emotionally. As a result, I liked being with people who had experienced gut-wrenching pain and done the hard work of therapy like I was doing.

They were real, and they didn't make me feel like I was the "odd" one.

Immediately, my heart warmed to Walt and his struggles. I had never known anyone who had battled and overcome so much, particularly with something as basic and essential as one's gender. Over the course of many conversations with Walt over several years, I became familiar with his world, one filled with the tragic unforeseen consequences of earlier choices.

When Cathy and I would meet Walt for an occasional breakfast, I'd hear his frustration spill out about his menial job, or at other times, his lack of job. I got used to hearing him say: "If only someone would give me a chance. I can do so many things." How he had so much more to give than baking muffins at a coffee shop. How he hated not making a living wage and having to depend on others for life's necessities. I was naive—why couldn't he get a good job and keep it? It sounded like just so much whining to me. Then he explained how the sections on the job application that were no problem for someone like me, loomed large for him because his job history bounced back and forth between two different names and genders. It was a minefield with no clear path through. I kept thinking that, with all his talents, Walt should work for himself, in his own business, but I didn't push it. He was single-mindedly determined to be accepted back into the corporate world.

Walt was Cathy's friend, so if the three of us got together, it was her idea. But Walt would insist on paying for our lunch. He didn't live close by, but rather than inconvenience us with the driving, he would insist on driving over to our side of the Bay. I was starting to feel an imbalance in our friendship. Due to my own bent toward co-dependency I was very much on alert about keeping a sense of equity in the effort of my friendships. It bugged me because I knew he was barely making ends meet. I needed to do something for him.

One Saturday afternoon, I picked up some burritos and drove to meet him at Ed's shop twenty-five miles away, where he was restoring a truck. He was blown away that anyone would drive so far to bring him lunch. We later referred to it as "the burrito experience." Walt says that's when he started to fall for me.

It's hard to remember the specifics of how our friendship grew, because it was so gradual and natural, never forced. I just knew he was easy to be with. It was a little bit like the taming of the fox in *The Little Prince* by Antoine de Saint Exupéry. Walt was a little skittish and months would pass without seeing him. Now with hindsight, I know that those were the "Laura" times.

When Walt rented his own apartment in a nearby town, Cathy suggested that we get some gifts and celebrate his ability to afford his own place. He proudly showed off his apartment, effusing over the generous gifts from a house-warming party given in his honor the week before by his supporters. The living room, sparsely furnished with one easy chair and a television, seemed a little lonely to me.

I've always been very conservative and practical in the cars I acquire. I kept my first car for ten years, and the second one for eight years. But all the counseling was having a freeing effect on me. When I saw a red convertible advertised at work, I decided to buy it. However, because I'm very practical and it was a used car, I wanted someone to check it over for me first. Cathy recommended that I call Walt— he was good with cars. On the phone I described the three-year-old Toyota Celica convertible with only 17,000 miles on it and asked if he would look it over for me. He was so funny: "That's a new car! Buy it!" With his encouragement, I became the proud owner of a bright red convertible.

It only seemed right that I show Walt the car. He had been so encouraging. After that our friendship grew, and I made sure that I always knew Walt's phone number, no matter where he moved—whether briefly at the apartment, or back at the Thompsons', or in Murphys, or in San Diego. I counted him among one of very few people that I totally trusted and could talk to about anything.

Then in the spring of 1996, at the age of 46, Cathy was diagnosed with terminal cancer. When I didn't know what to do or what to say to my best friend, I could count on Walt's wisdom. I so appreciated his friendship. We even prayed together; healing for Cathy, a job for Walt, and for me, a husband!

In December, I suggested to Walt that he and I do something fun together. We were always dwelling on Cathy's illness; how about a movie? He was living in Pleasanton with the Thompsons; and I again felt that he was doing all the driving in our friendship, so I insisted on driving the forty or so miles to Pleasanton. Afterwards, he took me to meet Bonita and Roy Thompson for the first time.

Bonita delights in telling the story of how she invited me to sit down, and rather than taking the empty single chair, I cleared the things off the loveseat next to where Walt was already sitting. Months later Walt told me that after I left, Bonita told him, "Watch out. She really likes you. She could have taken a seat anywhere, but she moved the laundry to sit next to you. Trust me; I'm never wrong about these things." Bonita was hearing wedding bells, and Walt and I hadn't even had a real date yet.

I only knew that I loved being with Walt. He was easy to be with. When I needed someone fun to go with me to my company's lavish Christmas party, I thought Walt would be perfect. I knew he would be appropriate and yet playful. At the entrance to the party, the coat-check clerk asked if we were a couple, and I quickly assured the clerk we were not a couple, just "buddies." Walt kidded me all night, "He only wanted to know whether to put the coats on the same ticket or not."

At Christmas time, when Walt insisted on taking me to the airport to catch my flight to see my family, and to pick me up when I returned, eighty miles round-trip from his home at the Thompsons' in Pleasanton, I began to think maybe he was getting sweet on me. Then he asked me out for my birthday, three weeks away. No friend had ever reserved my birthday that many weeks ahead. It started to dawn on me that Walt wanted to date, not just be friends.

I wanted to do everything in this relationship Christ's way, not my way. After eight years of being single and eight years of growing in my knowledge of Jesus, I had come to learn that I could only marry a man that fit the biblical description of a godly husband. And I wanted to make very sure Walt was that man before committing my heart to him, even for dating. I knew that if I were to toy with Walt's affections and date him without being open to the possibility of marriage, I would hurt him deeply when we parted ways. It was written all over his face. I did not want to inflict that kind of harm on my precious friend.

For the previous five or so years, with the assistance of an incredible Christian counselor, I had worked on resolving my childhood issues, growing in God's way of being single and developing healthy relationships. With her guidance a year earlier, I had developed a wish list of attributes that my ideal mate would possess. The lineup of traits was wide-ranging—39 items—and included such things as: pleasant attitude, kind to all, loves Jesus, laughs at himself, laughs with me, has close friends, gets over arguments easily, romantic, been through a small crisis and come out the other side, and so on. It was no surprise to me that Walt had 38 out of 39 items! Everyone always asks: "What was the other one?" I'll tell you—it was skiing. Right then and there I decided I could be happy in life without ever skiing again.

In the light of such overwhelming evidence that Walt was God's answer to my prayers, I arranged for him to meet my counselor. With his permission, I shared his history with her privately so she could give her honest opinion of us based on knowing everything. After spending time with us together, seeing us interact, and answering her questions, she expressed her delight with the match-up. Later she told me that she could see that the Lord would use each of us to complete the healing in the other. And that has proven to be so very true. Unconditional love is a powerful healing force.

Of course, Walt and I had to discuss the very important physical issues. I asked Walt, "Does it matter to you that I'm taller than you?" He answered, "No, does it bother you that I'm shorter than you?" And that simple declaration was the end of any concern about my being two inches taller. And in that same simplicity of heart, with God's grace, and through our mutual unconditional love, other differences that might have mattered a great deal have mattered not at all.

Walt was embarrassed that his chest bore the scars of previous surgeries. My response was that all people get scarred in life; he just happened to have his scars on the outside. They didn't matter to me. His scarred chest is simply a reminder of how fierce the battle was that he had waged most of his life.

Since our wedding, we have developed an easy way of relating, and we complement the strengths and weaknesses of one other. Walt is the visionary and I'm the detailed task-master. Some of the most satisfying times in our marriage have been those when we worked together on a project.

For example, we developed our own self-storage business from the ground up. Walt's business instincts, honed during his car-business days, gave him the vision for where and what the business could be. My business degree and career in the computer industry gave me a sense for the practical details of budget and financing, and the computer needs. We spent months working together to make the vision a reality.

It was extremely satisfying to see the business succeed due to our efforts, and the experience gave us a deeper appreciation and love for the other.

In our twelve years of marriage, I've seen Walt "kick so much old baggage down the hill." Roadblocks that formerly stood in his way have disappeared through his hard work and determination to try. I always thought he'd do well in his own business, and he proved me right! He later sold our successful self-storage business at a profit. Then he bought a "fixer-upper" condo and completely gutted and updated it, with stunning results.

One accomplishment that eluded Walt during his early years of recovery was to successfully gain employment with a major corporation, even if it was only an entry-level position. He was reluctant to try due to the many painful rejections in the past. But when a major hotel chain in our area held a job fair to solicit employees for their new timeshare resort, I encouraged him to go and submit his application. It would be a tell-tale sign whether or not his past history still blocked his way. Imagine our celebration when Walt was selected for guardhouse duty at the entry gate, a full-time job with benefits! Recovery from the past is measured in such small but significant successes. And now recently, as you know, the Lord really outdid himself by matching up Walt with a director position at church that utilizes his skills at a high level. That was the ultimate career redemption.

Laboring together on this book has been very fulfilling. Walt wrote while I edited and organized it. We've felt the Lord's blessing as we've pushed through to the finish. My prayer is that the Lord will show you how to apply the truths found here to expand your own heart's capacity to love the people God has placed around you, and to never lose trust that God will answer your prayers.

Love never gives up, never loses faith, is always hopeful, and endures through every circumstance.
(1 Corinthians 13:7, NLT)

God can do anything, you know—far more than you could ever imagine or guess or request in your wildest dreams! He does it not by pushing us around but by working within us, His Spirit deeply and gently within us.
(Ephesians 3:20, The Message Bible)

Chapter 13

Finishing Thoughts

For years I have said, "Don't take life too seriously because you're not going to live through it anyway. Love the Lord and family, looking as often as you can at the bright side, the fun stuff."

Sure, I had some tough times but it was not all bad. I also had some very fun and exciting times. I worked on the Apollo space missions projects and built a small mini storage business with my wonderful wife, Kaycee. I have shaken the hand of Richard M. Nixon, former president of the United States. Also, the hands of James Cash Penny, founder of J.C. Penny, and Roger Penske, owner of Hertz-Penske Trucking and board member of Home Depot, whose auto racing teams have won the Indianapolis 500 and in 2008 the NASCAR big event, the Daytona 500.

I picked up Roger Penske at the Dallas airport in 1969 as his personal chauffer from American Motors Corporation for the weekend. Roger was under contract with American Motors to develop a racing team for the Trans-American Sedan Championship (Trans-Am). He was in Dallas that particular weekend to lend his celebrity and that of his famous driver, Johnny Rutherford, three-time winner of the Indy 500, to the opening of a new raceway. That day I got the ride of my life—over 140 miles per hour in a Camaro modified for Trans-Am racing driven by Johnny Rutherford. I can tell you that that ride, especially in the racetrack curves, was an adrenalin rush I will not forget.

On another occasion, for a national dealer event in San Diego, I was designated to pick up the president of American Motors at the airport. His name was George Romney. (His son Mitt ran in the 2008 presidential primaries.) I remember when the event was over, as we were pulling away from the hotel, a reporter starting pounding on the window. He wanted an interview with the company president. Mr. Romney said, "Okay, but get in the car and you can interview me on the way to the airport. This young man (pointing at me) will bring you back to the hotel." That was cool stuff to a guy in his twenties.

Another fun thing I did was call the Rush Limbaugh radio show, and success came one morning when I was living in Murphys and drawing disability. Rush was going on and on about the people who live off the state and will not get up and do everything possible to get a job. I wanted to explain to him that for people like me, an alcoholic transsexual, there were no jobs. We could not get work like normal people.

To my surprise I got through the screening process and there I was voice-to-voice with the legend El Rushbo. I went into my tale of poor me and scorned him for coming off so tough on people like me. Rush said, "You live near Sacramento don't you?" I said, "Yes." Then he followed with, "If you really want to work you will go to Sacramento and walk into every building—high rise and low rise—and tell them you want a job, you will do anything. That is how you get work." Rush went on to say, "You will not get a job sitting at home talking about your alcoholism or life's failures."

I said my thanks and hung up the phone. Having Rush Limbaugh's voice in my head telling me what I knew to be true and what I did not want to hear was convicting. That call with Rush initiated a desire in me to get off disability and go back and try even harder to find work. I knew Rush was right; yes, he is way right, but he is mostly truthful.

Another thing that is cool is I still visit with Jeff Farrar, Roy Thompson and most of the others who were so important to my restoration and recovery. What I learned was unmistakable; that is how profoundly and skillfully the Lord uses His people in such detail. I had lost touch with Reverend Bob Kraning, the kind pastor from Forest Home who had counseled my family during the time of my alcoholic transsexual disaster. But then unexpectedly, the Lord put our paths together once again. Here is how that came about.

A few years ago our church was without a senior pastor and needed one to preach for the interim period. Imagine my goose bumps when I heard that the person selected was someone I knew, but I hadn't seen or talked to in twenty years. It was Bob Kraning, whom I had gotten to know some thirty years earlier at Forest Home Christian Conference Center, and who had worked so hard in vain to prevent my disaster. What would he think now?

I alerted him ahead of time via email that he would see me at the church and tried to fill in the gaps since he had last seen me. I expressed my delight at being able to visit with him and his wife, Carol, once again, only this time he would see first-hand the restoration the Lord had done in my life. When Bob received my email, he immediately picked up the phone and called me. He was very curious and eager to hear how everything turned out. In typical Bob fashion, he remembered and asked about the rest of my family. He and I made a date to get together with our wives after that weekend's Saturday service.

I went early that Saturday night. I was nervous, with sweaty palms, my senses a little on edge, since I had not seen Bob for over twenty years. In the dimly lit sanctuary, I waited. About a hundred feet away, I saw the backlit figure of a man walking from the bright sunshine into the darkened room. The silhouette was unmistakably Bob Kraning walking directly toward me. He didn't recognize me. In a friendly fashion, he stuck out his hand and said, "Hi, I'm Bob Kraning." "I'm Walt Heyer," I replied, and we fell into a big bear hug of recognition, love and tears. Bob knew I was an incredible living example of the power, love, and grace of Jesus Christ who restores broken lives.

As we sized up the changes twenty years had wrought in the other's appearance, the first thing I said was, "Bob, I was a little screwed up the last time you saw me." Bob in a louder than normal voice, with a jaunty smile, replied, "Ya think?!" It was so perfect a response on his part, and put me at ease.

What serendipity—encountering Bob who was so pivotal in earlier, painful times of my life, and having the opportunity to show him how my life had been restored. I will always mark this as a miraculous event in my life.

I loved being a dad to my son and daughter when they were growing up; we had fun. As a young family, going to Forest Home Christian Conference Center was a summer highlight for all of us. My kids continue to be amazing and wonderful gifts to me.

My high school class of '58 continues to get together on a regular basis, sometimes traveling as a group to visit various classmates who now live in other states. The class continues to grow closer and closer as time goes by.

The truth is: life is good, real good.

My desire for you, when you have closed the cover on the last page of this story, is that you'll be inspired, excited, and filled with joy for the possibilities the Lord has for each of us, no matter how broken our lives may have become. Remember Jesus has the glue to put all the little pieces back better than ever, but you need to come under His care for that possibility to take place. I am a living example of His powerful amazing love. The world will let you down if that is where you turn for wisdom and truth.

Also, remember to be careful about whom you reject. They could become one more trophy of grace, a care director or even a world famous author. It all can happen when you place a broken life into the loving hands of the Master. I love you all. Thanks for taking this journey with me. Until next time, remember to love everyone, even or especially the ones you do not like. They, too, have the potential to become trophies of grace when placed in the loving hands of the Master.

We are very thankful that this is a success story. A story of hope. And above all, a story of an all-loving Father and the amazing grace of His Son, Jesus.

As Catherine Martin expressed in her forward, Walt is aptly described as a "Trophy of God's Grace." And in the midst of life's journey, I was fortunate to find a friend for life.
—Dr. Roy Thompson

References
Fresh Wind, Fresh Fire, Jim Cymbala with Dean Merrill,
Zondervan Publishing, 1997

More Information
Please visit www.tradingmysorrows.com and
www.sexchangeregret.com.

Contact Information
To contact the author, send email to
waltsbook@yahoo.com.

CPSIA information can be obtained
at www.ICGtesting.com
Printed in the USA
LVHW091140060322
712759LV00020B/170